I0073973

Life in 4-Part Harmony

Get *Everything* in Your Life to Work With *Everything Else* in Your Life

SANDRA Y. LEWIS

Life in 4-Part Harmony
Get Everything in Your Life
To Work With Everything Else in Your Life
By Sandra Y. Lewis

ISBN: 978-1-937392-01-7

Sandra Y. Lewis
The Living Source
Montclair, New Jersey
www.Lifein4PartHarmony.com
(973) 509-8017

Published by
Oshun Golden Harvest Publishing
Montclair, New Jersey

Dedication

For Mama and Daddy who loved me into life.

Acknowledgements

Mama Louise, Mother and Mama Stewart thank you for stirring my commitment to serve others and build a better world. Words don't quite capture my gratitude for the way my family loves me into greater expressions of my purpose. I'm thankful to the intersecting circles of women, friends, mentors, and everyday warriors who help me take big and little steps forward on my business mission. To Queen Bishop, Iya, and Grand Master, your spiritual counsel is an ever-present catalyst for the faith I need to stay the course. Sue Toth, my editor, your attention to detail, nudges, and push for clarity were the perfect touch. Marty Marsh, thank you for the visible and invisible work you did to help me transform my vision into tangible reality.

Table of Contents

Thank you for purchasing my book, Life In 4-Part Harmony

You're ready to get *everything* in your life to work with *everything else* your life. As we know, this will take energy – physical, mental, emotional and spiritual energy. You've already answered the "Call to Action" so let's get started.

Visit this link to access your
free bundle of worksheets:
thelivingsource.lpages.co/l4pharmony/

Make your life sing with strategies to:

1. Energize your body, mind and spirit.
2. Maximize your performance and productivity.
3. Elevate your life satisfaction.

Find your glow. Live in your flow with Life in 4-Part Harmony.

Peace & Blessings

Sandra

Preface

I grew up surrounded by women that I would eventually perceive as magical. They went about nurturing families, going to work, sometimes working two jobs, and playing an active role in their communities. Despite daily challenges to their identity, they found their place in the world. Often buffeted about by racism, sexism, and classism, they had to manage a number of health and wellness challenges. Yet, they stayed connected to what truly sustained them each day. Their faith and their enduring sense of meaningfulness in their daily lives were their infinite resource. They are the subjects of June Jordan's poem *Oughta be a Woman* that Sweet Honey in the Rock sang so beautifully. The poem describes the endless tasks of a woman who is emotional support for everyone, including people who devalue her. She's expected to be all things to all people, to solve all the problems that come her way. While the poem highlights her courage, it raises questions about her needs. Jordan points out that there should be a way for her to take a break, break down even, and to simply sit down. These two lines end the poem:

A way outa no way is too much to ask
Too much of a task for any one woman

Most of us have multiple roles. We often take the just get it all done approach, barreling through our day fueled by a caffeinated breakfast or a green drink here and there. There are days when we know it's too much to ask. We're often excellent organizers, good time managers. But we may pay very little attention to our physical, mental, emotional, and spiritual energy needs. Okay, maybe we go to church on Sunday or a yoga class or we work out three times per week. Perhaps, we plan a great vacation once or twice a year. We renew ourselves but then we get right back to breaking ourselves down.

And we pass this way of living from one generation to the next. Each generation seems well-prepared to exist on too little sleep and attempt to thrive on "energy" drinks. This formula won't produce lasting fulfillment or happiness. It may lead us to discomfort in our body, mind, and spirit. As many of us know, our body will simply start saying no until we're forced to stop, take a break, and recover.

But what if recovery and renewal were part of every day? What if we had simple strategies to build personal renewal into what we do each day? The magical women in my life knew their life was a gift defined by divine purpose. They taught me that connecting to an infinite source is the key to living with meaning and sustaining a well-defined sense of self no matter what challenges you face. I learned that resilience requires inner power.

So, here's a question for you. What if we paid as much attention to the energy we need to get things done as we do to making it all happen?

Imagine the things you'll do, the places you'll go, and how good you will feel.

When Life Throws You Off Your Beat

Last night a DJ saved my life. Last night a DJ saved my life from a broken heart. Last night a DJ saved my life with a song.
~ InDeep

I've heard many women talk about how they used music in their lives. I grew up watching my Mama move to everything from jazz to gospel to rhythm and blues. Every one of them offered something different for her soul. Like an interview I once listened to with a woman who talked about her relationship with music. She had music for cleaning the house, music for troubled times, etc. Her patterns were so clear that her family knew if they walked in and heard gospel music, they needed to give her some space. She was in the midst of working something out and should not be disturbed except in matters of life or death. Like many of us, she used music to find her beat again, to reconnect with her source, that power center within where you can find all the answers about your next best move.

Life sometimes throws us off beat. We might lose our rhythm because of a major life change like a sick relative or new job, or it might be one of those everyday hassles like being the problem solver that everyone at home and work looks to for answers. However, they rarely come with support for you.

One of the roughest times in my life came as I was catching up on some work and the phone rang. It was my cousin calling to say that one of my favorite aunties was very ill, very likely dealing with a terminal illness.

This is the auntie who used her design and sewing skills to make my prom dress and a suit that I wore to an important interview. When she was a teenager and I was a little girl sharing a bed with her and my other auntie, she tolerated my knees in her back and my toes in her face. Soon into this phone call, I was crying, worried. Later, I called other family members and the more I talked the more I realized that I wanted to get home to Atlanta. But when? How? What do I rearrange?

Mix the weight of the sadness and anxiety that I felt with all the priorities demanding my attention, like research, writing, and managing a business. Then add the task of reorganizing so that I could travel to spend time with my aunt and family, and I was overwhelmed. Completely overwhelmed.

I was waking up feeling drained because I didn't sleep well. I was sad. I was moving through my day heavy, getting the major things done but really falling behind on some creative projects. So now, I was starting to question myself and wonder, "Why did I get into these things anyway? I'm always doing too much."

In this moment, I was emotionally distraught. I was using the bulk of my energy to manage my sadness and anxiety. My worry. My fear of losing my aunt. My fear of not being able to say, "I love you," to her while she was still coherent and able to feel my love for her.

The emotional weight of the experience completely filled center stage. But recovery would require my body, mind, and spirit to work as a team. My body was suffering from emotional overstimulation. My thoughts were racing. And I was having difficulty accessing my spiritual wisdom. It always saves me. It always gets me back on recovery road.

Clearly, I needed a change. I was fading. I had to revive myself. So, I began the process by rearranging my morning routine. I spent more time in early morning meditation, prayer, and Qigong. This helped me face the day with greater strength and resolve. Throughout the day, I spent more time breathing. Yes, simply breathing.

I ended the day in the same way I started. I meditated or practiced Qigong so that I could sleep better. Good and replenishing rest was the fix for the physical and emotional fatigue that I was feeling. I needed my physical vitality in order to get through this experience with more mental and emotional energy. I needed my body at its best so that I could think more clearly and process my experience.

Crying whenever the tears came was an important part of my revival. I cried when I needed to. I called my family and cried on the phone. I listened to the feelings of loss and love contained in my tears. And I realized how the concerns about loss led me to notice the love, a lifetime of love that was mine to keep.

And the wisdom my mother bestowed upon me during childhood was a calming refrain during this difficult and disturbing time. "God don't put no more on you than you can bear." I've come to understand that this Mama Wisdom isn't an order to suck it up and bear the pain. Though some treat it as a directive to be strong and show how much pain you can take and never let anyone see you sweat, it's not a call to martyrdom.

Rather, it's a reminder that we have all the resources we need in any situation. They may not always be obvious to us. But we have exactly what it takes to manage the downs and rise to the top so that we can operate with more comfort. We can navigate rough waters when we free up enough energy to find our rhythm and go with the flow.

My spiritual beliefs helped me ground myself. Once I quieted my mind and emotions, I asked myself, "What does this situation need?" The answer came back loudly and clearly, "Love." If my aunt was in the final part of her life, she needed to feel love and peace, and so did I. I had to come to the realization that the love she and I shared all of my life would survive illness and death. In fact, it would sustain us both.

I thought very clearly about how she'd helped me become the person I am today. She's deep in my foundation. She is a part of the family that keeps me standing strong in my purpose and my commitment to women and families. She played a major role in my love of joy and all things beautiful, my sense of style and willingness to redefine ordinary and normal.

My guess is that you're also familiar with rough times. You know what it's like to feel you're at your edge. Major life events like my experience with my aunt make it easy for us to say, "It's time to take a step back," or "Let me revive myself," or "I need some recovery time." But we often let the everyday disruptions to our well-being and productivity go unattended. We'll move about our day feeling drained or as though something just isn't right, but we may not stop to tend to our needs.

- Maybe you're overwhelmed dealing with a sick relative and taking care of your children and managing your career.
- Maybe you're the problem solver in your family and at work and people always come to you for answers, but they never come with support.
- Maybe you have a project that's really important, and you're losing your confidence. You're doubting yourself. You're stalling. You can't move forward on it.
- Maybe you find that you're always in push-push mode. You're getting things done. There's no white space in your calendar but you're wondering, "What the heck does any of this have to do with who I came to the world to be?"

If so, this book is for you. On the surface, this book seems to be about self-care, personal energy management, and/or wellness. You're right. That's true. It's about all of those things. But why? Because these things are an unequivocal source of power for our personal why, our reason for being, that special sauce that we add to everything we touch.

Each of us has some unique talents and a distinct purpose that can light up our lives, families, communities, and the world. You may be in charge of many people and activities. But the light that we call, "you," is the driver in your relationships and everything you do. These are the missions that give you space to uplift your voice, your talents, your good stuff into the world. This requires energy of every kind, physical, mental, emotional, and spiritual.

The deck is stacked in our favor. We come well-equipped with a body, mind, and spirit that are capable of renewal and recovery. In fact, expending energy, replenishing, and recovery is a process that we use to grow and to expand. Our body, mind, and spirit seek alignment with each other. When we're aligned, we have that just right feeling, an inner harmony that extends into everything we do. We can bring our best to what matters most. I guarantee you that expressing your purpose in the world is one of the things that matters most.

Desmond Tutu describes Ubuntu, a Zulu philosophy about the universal connection that sustains all life. He says, "I want you to be all that you can be. I need you to be you so that I can be me." We've got many roles and jobs and things to do. Each one of them is our opportunity to embody the good we came to share with the world.

How can you be all that you can be? Fulfill your life purpose. It's a beat written into your spirit. You've had it all the time. Fulfilling your purpose in the world is what makes your heart sing.

Let's get on the beat.

What Does It Take?

We are stardust brought to life, then empowered by the universe to figure itself out – and we've only just begun.
~ Neil deGrasse Tyson, Astrophysicist

This is a question that we've asked ourselves about one thing or another. What does it take to get things done? What do I need to make it all happen? How can I win at life without losing myself? What's the secret ingredient to joy, success, happiness, ease, or any other good thing that we might crave?

The simple response is energy. I'd add -- all kinds of energy. You need your body, thoughts, emotions, and spirit working as a unit. Your body, mind, and spirit need to be ready, willing, and able to power your purpose, that beat that makes your heart sing.

Performance and productivity experts like Jim Loehr of the Johnson and Johnson Human Performance Institute say that managing energy, not time, is the secret to being fully engaged. In our everyday experience, this might look like being comfortable putting your phone away while you enjoy lunch with friends or colleagues. Or being completely mesmerized by your child's soccer game or dance recital, even though you have a big meeting with a potential client the next day. Or spending 15 minutes reading a novel the first thing every morning and feeling completely intrigued by what's happening with the characters in the book. Or easily focusing on a proposal, plan, blog post, or other writing project and feeling your ideas come effortlessly.

Engagement. Readiness. Flow. Presence. Can you feel it? It's what my mother was creating when she taught me to get my clothes and book bag ready at night. Minimize distractions so that you can maximize your resources. Create some ease and flow in the world around you so that you can have ease and flow inside. This is why many productivity experts recommend creating a workspace that invites you to be creative and generate meaningful work.

And when I was a kid, we had recess. This was a space in the middle of the day when we got to play, to explore the world using our bodies and imagination. Then we went back to work. We learned to take a break when we had trouble with a math problem. Do something else and then come back to it. The time away often got our mental memory juices simmering, and we could solve the problem when we came back to it.

Our ability to be fully present and engaged depends on a cycle of expending and replenishing our energy. The trick is to make replenishing and recharging a part of our lives. If we were smart phones, we'd have gauges to remind us of our energy level.

I used to associate being, "in the red," with being over budget, not having enough funds to manage demands. Thanks to smarty-pants phones, I also associate this phrase with my phone. It's a loud and clear message that, "I'm going to quit you, if you don't plug me in." It even warns me: "low battery."

Some devices offer battery stretch or low power mode. The phone will ask me, "Do you want to continue in low power mode?" Yep. It's a smarty-pants who knows how to give you a message with just a hint of sarcasm. This message could just as easily say, "Only a foolish person would choose to operate in low power mode. But if you've had some drastic circumstance that prohibited charging me, go ahead, this is your best choice."

But I really do not like seeing these messages on my phone. In fact, they leave me feeling a bit delinquent, like I haven't properly attended to my phone's energy needs. That little bit of sarcasm that I hear works.

You can probably understand this feeling, if you grew up with a mother like mine. She taught me, "Never go to bed with less than ¼ tank of gas in your car." This strategy was a part of her readiness approach to life. Simply put, organize your life so that you are ready, able to respond when called.

I know some used to say, it's better to let your phone's battery go to the lowest point before recharging it. This was prescribed as a strategy that improved battery efficiency. That's fine. And it might work well if you're always near a power source. But when my phone is in the red, I don't like it.

I don't like it when I feel low on energy either. If I wait until I'm in the red, I'm probably sick. Since we don't have red lights or low battery messages flashing on our foreheads, we need other ways of getting this information.

Sometimes it's that, "I think I might be coming down with something" feeling. Other times, it's an ache in our lower back. Maybe our necks or shoulders feel tense. And if we let it go too far, we may feel drained or even numb. Just like our cell phone, we need to plug in and recharge our energy. Downtime is in order.

Just like our phones, we're energy networks. Our eyes, ears, and skin are picking up signals from the world around us. We've got neurons sending signals to each other. We soak up sunlight and get an infusion of Vitamin D. We use energy to power our bodies, thoughts, and emotions. We need to find ways to keep it flowing smoothly.

A long line of elders taught me that possibility is a combination of what we can see and what we can't. The power behind what we see and do determines our course. We don't see the power going into our phones or computers. But we know we won't be able to use these devices without it. What's possible for our bodies, minds, and spirits depends on what we don't see. But we definitely feel energy.

The idea that everything takes energy is as ancient as the idea that everything is energy. My Taoist Qigong Grand Master and Chinese medicine scholar, Dr. Nan Lu, describes our internal energy system as our, "inner-net". He explains our body as a network of meridians or pathways that carry energy to and fro. These pathways map onto our major organs. They support everything we do, from movement to digestion to emotional experiences and connecting to the unlimited energy in nature and our universe.

Physicists say that we're made of star stuff. Check out this definition of a star from freedictionary.com.

> *A celestial body that generates light and other radiant energy and consists of a mass*

> *of gas held together by its own gravity in which the energy generated by nuclear reactions in the interior is balanced by the outflow of energy to the surface, and the inward-directed gravitational forces are balanced by the outward-directed gas and radiation pressures.*

Stars generate energy. They have an internal process that holds them together. This system is based on balancing internal actions with energy outflow. The star's outward actions balance the forces impinging on the star.

You see why physicists say that we're stardust? Stars generate energy expressed as light. They balance their inflow and outgo so that they can keep it all together.

Physicists also remind us that energy supports all forms of matter. The energy beneath the atoms is full of unlimited possibility. Possibility is what we're aiming to create in our everyday lives. We're looking for what it takes, what makes it possible to make everything in our lives work and play well together. We're looking for ways to create harmony among our many roles. We want the mom, career woman, entrepreneur, daughter, partner, spouse, runner, and yogi to get along with each other.

We look for ways to have it all feel just right. Everything fits just right. Like your favorite jeans. Just right. And the best thing about this harmony is that it opens the way for growth and expansion. It creates movement. Like a star, we can power our possibility.

The Africans of ancient Kemet (now called Egypt) gifted us the concept, Maat, to explain this process. Maat is the force of nature, the energy source that creates and sustains harmony. It's one of her cardinal principles. Egyptologist Rkhty Amen describes Maat as the, "harmonious balance, the agreement and adaptation of all the various parts/elements of creation to form a connected whole," (p 12, 2012). I think of her as the force that makes sure everything works with everything else.

Take a minute. Think about this. These wise ones from this ancient culture with 10,000 years of documented history left us a message about the driving force behind the harmony that governs the whole universe, the stars, planets, rain, people, plants, dirt, fish, trees. All the stuff that we see and know and things that we can't see and don't know are part of a universal web, ordering and balancing itself to maintain harmony.

If we follow that "As Above So Below Law," the first thing we can learn from Maat is that harmony requires energy. You need energy to get everything to work with everything else. It takes energy to keep it all together. And as Oprah says, you know that for sure.

One of the best things about ancient traditions is that they don't leave us wondering how to put the science into action. That is, how to get the heavenly laws to work in our everyday life. Maat is science, philosophy, spirituality, and lifestyle practices. She shows us how to create the energy that sustains harmony, that, "It's so right" feeling. In fact, Amen says the pharaoh was a spiritual leader of sorts and maintaining Maat was his sole concern. Imagine that, the leader's job is to sustain harmony. Pharaohs and their servant leadership team put Maat into practice, providing guidance on everything from good table manners to personal development to self-monitoring one's thoughts and emotions and much more.

Maat's cardinal principles provide us with guidelines. I put them into a simple formula that I call Life In 4-Part Harmony:

Truth + Order + Balance + Reciprocity = Harmony

These four principles of Maat tune us in to our power source. Yes, it's the power to make things happen.

And it is the power to use stillness, to know when to slow down, to manage and renew our resources. When we practice Maat, we can get into our flow and keep it going. We find our rhythm and stay in tune. No matter what happens around us or what life demands of us, we have an infinite power source that we can access to give exactly what the situation needs.

- ***Truth*** **guides our commitment to our unique, divine life purpose. We honor our deepest, most authentic self when we speak truth and do truth.** ***Truth*** **connects us to our values, integrity and inner knowing.**
- ***Order*** **reminds us of the importance of synchronicity as well as strategy. There is a time for everything. Everything in time.** ***Order*** **brings to light integration among aspects of our lives as well as alignment of our body, mind and spirit.** ***Order*** **allows the parts of the whole to move and operate in relationship to each other.**
- ***Balance*** **reveals the power of complementary forces that cultivate stability as well as movement. Hot and cold are polar energies that can create a warm and cozy place.** ***Balance*** **brings attention to monitoring,**

prioritizing, and spending our resources wisely. *Balance* hinges on knowing when and how to shift.

- ***Reciprocity* refers to unity and linkages among things. It is both the practice of sharing good with others and being grateful for what we have. *Reciprocity* reminds us that a better world happens because we make it so. We thrive because of our inter-relations with all life.**
- ***Harmony* is the, "Mmmm good," place where everything is just right. It's like a perfect forkful of food with all the flavors working together. It's when everything is working with everything else. When you're connecting to your truth, ordering your steps to get things done, moderating your energy expenditures, and noticing the gifts of your experiences, you're in *harmony*. Things flow very naturally and easily in this place. The value of every part is clear as well as its relationship to the whole.**

Each principle, Truth, Order, Balance, and Reciprocity offers some daily lifestyle guidelines, practices and strategies. Maat is a loving Mama. This feminine philosophy, science and spiritual teacher is committed to showing us how to light up like the stars we are every day. She's ready and willing to open the way for us to make our lives sing to the beat of our divine purpose.

When we use our inner wisdom, we put Truth into action. We have to ability to self-monitor our inner world and make assessments of the outer world. We're energy beings, capable of reading and interpreting signals. We can use this information to make decisions that sustain us, support our thriving from day to day and bring meaning into our lives.

Order in action is creating rhythm. It's planning to get that, "well-oiled machine," or "perfect tempo," effect as we go about executing our tasks. We engage in preventive and restorative activities. Order is responsiveness to our experiences, effective and efficient problem-solving. We pace ourselves as we move through our day, meeting and managing our activities.

Flexibility is an essential strategy for practicing balance. This means we need to become good human resource managers. Our ability to adapt is based upon energy demands, needs, and expenditures. It's an awareness that the ups and downs work as a team to help us create momentum or consistency. Balance in action is our ability to moderate and modulate our resources as our experiences change.

Reciprocity in action is using the power of connection within ourselves and with the world around us. There's an intimate feedback loop between our body, thoughts, emotions, and behavior that can energize us. We are intimately connected to people and living beings. These relationships also energize us. Giving and receiving in our relationships support ongoing renewal and replenishment.

Harmony in action is cultivating deep satisfaction. Positive psychologists call it flow. Athletes and others call it the zone. Our actions are informed by a deep sense of meaning and integration. We're able to give and be nurtured simultaneously. We're mindful of our inner world as well as peacefully and passionately engaged with our outer world. We're in the moment supported by our past and intrigued by what's possible. Everything, even seeming contradictions, fits. Both the forest and the trees make sense.

In the pages that follow, we will employ four strategies: Wisdom, Rhythm, Flexibility and Connection to build physical, mental, emotional and spiritual energy. Our aim is to build the energy we need to support our flow, our daily harmony, our sense of deep satisfaction. And ultimately, we light up the universe with our purpose.

It's Time to Check In

Start by taking a breath. You are a magnificent being. You're a living quilt of talents, gifts, feelings, thoughts, abilities, questions, strengths, challenges, and insights all perfectly blended into a unique pattern. You have tremendous capacity for growth, change, and transformation. When you unfurl your genius, you warm the world in your own special way.

We know that your genius needs a power source, energy. Our personal energy is an essential resource for productivity, wellness, full engagement, and life satisfaction. The team at the Johnson and Johnson Human Performance Institute has a long history of training and coaching people to manage their energy. Along with other scholars, they describe four types of energy: 1) Physical energy; 2) Mental energy; 3) Emotional energy; and 4) Spiritual energy.

Many of us think of energy as a resource for our bodies. But right away, these four categories make it clear that your body, mind, and spirit require energy. For me, the magic of it all is that you can use your body, mind, and spirit to generate energy. You're literally a living source of energy. When we're doing well, our energy is operating on a cycle that balances expenditures with refueling. Build energy. Expend energy. Rest. Recover. Replenish energy. Expend, rest, recover, replenish. This cycle is essential for all types of energy. The four types of energy work together as an integrated whole with each one supporting the others.

Physical energy refers to our sense of vitality. Loehr and Schwartz remind us that even if we spend most of our time in sedentary work, we need physical energy to stay upright and maintain good posture. We need our bodies operating with a good energy supply, because our physical self supports everything we do. It's our house. Our brains, muscles, joints, and organ systems facilitate alertness, creativity, focus, stress management, and sustained commitment to a goal as well as overall physical well-being. Our body requires regular infusions of energy such as food, water, and air. It benefits from movement, rest, sleep, breathing, and activities that aid in recovery. The body has a signaling system and will let us know when it's in need. The body also has self-regulating abilities and will use processes like breathing to regroup during times of stress or strain. Breath is an automatic function that we can take control of to create a shift and restore our body's and mind's energy supply.

Mental energy refers to our ability to focus, problem solve, make key decisions and adjust our mindset. Our ability to concentrate, actively engage with a task, interact in a conversation, or engross ourselves in a project all hinge on our mental energy. Cognitive skills require good sleep and vitality. Fatigue inhibits our ability to pay attention and be present in the moment. Our mindset is also a key component of mental energy. In today's world, just about everyone from psychologists to coaches to spiritual teachers and hair stylists listening to your worries is talking about mindset. As a child, my mother regularly quoted the bible verse, "As a man thinks so is he." Early in life, she taught me the power of my mindset. A simple change in perspective can create a significant upsurge in our mental, emotional, and physical energy.

Emotional energy refers to our ability to manage stress, modulate our emotional flow, and use our emotional wisdom to navigate life's ups and downs. Emotional intelligence was first coined by Salovey and Mayer and popularized by Daniel Goleman. It refers to our ability to notice, access, accurately detect, and utilize emotions for our growth and development. It's our capacity for empathy and using our emotions to facilitate meaningful social interactions. Our emotions help us connect within, to others and to our activities. They're intimately tied to our thoughts and bodies. While our nervous systems and thoughts generate our emotional responses, an increase or decrease in our overall energy may be associated with a particular emotional state. A significant amount of research and everyday life experience demonstrates how our feelings power our actions and choices. When we're well-fueled, we can effectively use our emotions as signals and guides through our experience. Because our emotions are such good partners with our minds and bodies, a shift in our thoughts or breathing will create a shift our emotional state.

Spiritual energy refers to our purpose and meaning, fulfillment that extends beyond personal gains, and a sense of connection to life. Our ability to see past our personal needs and comprehend interrelations among people, nature, and life is a core aspect of spiritual energy. Spiritual teachers, even physicists, would very likely say that our spirit, the intelligence beneath our physical matter, is our central energy source. Many traditions describe the spirit as infinite intelligence that incarnates in a physical form for a specific purpose. Sobonfu Somé says that we are all born with a purpose and our interactions in community and the world help us to manifest it. In our everyday experience, spiritual energy is a yearning to make a difference in the world or in our families. It's a desire for meaning and fulfillment. It's a sense that we have a significant role to play in our universe. However, a purpose is not a specific job or career. It's our way of sharing our talents with the world, which can take place in a job or a supermarket checkout line. It's the ultimate understanding of the ripple or pay it forward effect. When we share good with others, they're moved to continue sharing with those they encounter.

So, how's your energy? Do you feel fully charged? Are there some energy leaks that need plugging? Are you replenishing? Is your energy input keeping up with your energy output? How's your recovery plan? What are your primary sources of energy? Personal energy management is one of the most powerful actions we can take on our behalf and on behalf of those we encounter from day to day. When we're not doing the best job of "expend, rest, recover, and replenish," our bodies, minds, and spirits will send us a signal.

Below are some of the ways that we get stressed, strained, drained, overwhelmed, or stuck in a groove that won't let us move. Which ones have you been friends with at one time or another? Is there one that's currently at the top of your list? Maybe there are some others that you would add to this list. Feel free to list them in your journal. Make this fun.

- ***Problem-Solving Pro*** - being so good at creating solutions that others think you don't need help.
    - This Pro excels at helping others manage their difficulties. They're so good at wearing their skills that others think they're invincible. Often, they think they will let others down if they show their vulnerabilities.
- ***Managing Mogul*** - providing care and direction to multiple people and projects but not asking for help.
    - The Mogul makes multiple roles and multitasking a way of life. They often get caught up thinking that they have to do everything on their own. They may fear or be ashamed of making requests of others. They may also believe that, "If you want something done, you have to do it yourself."
- ***Deferred Dreamer*** - putting your goals on the back burner until the water boils out of them.
    - The Deferrer will put others' goals before their own. Often their self-doubts,

misconceptions about failure, their anxiety about getting started or their perfectionism hinder their willingness to move on their dreams.

- ***Detail Dictator*** - stalled because you're absorbed by the details.
  - The Dictator sweats the small stuff. They tend to overanalyze and get paralyzed. They want everything to be perfect and often won't take action until they think nothing will go wrong. They tend to see delays or setbacks as hindrances rather than assistants.
- ***Robot on Skates*** - moving so much that you feel off/worried when you slow down.
  - The Robot keeps busy. When they slow down, they get concerned that something is going undone. They wear busy as a badge of honor. They often lose sight of the relationship between their actions and their purpose, meaning, fulfillment.
- ***Ruminating Worrier*** - questioning and second-guessing your goals, decisions or actions.
  - The worrier gets stuck in a loop of thoughts and emotions. Their internal dialogue makes it difficult for them to trust

themselves. Even when others congratulate or praise them, they're likely to wonder if it's, "good enough."

- ***Drained Doer*** - working and busy staying on your grind.
    - The Doer sometimes wakes up to discover they're still dressed or holding their laptop in their lap. They fully believe in working overtime. They may ask for help, but they're likely to think that little sleep and poor eating are necessary for success. They may not recognize their body's signals for food or rest. They may only stop when they get sick.

These patterns, along with many others, are indications that we're not managing our energy well. Patterns take time to develop. Clues that we may be going in the wrong direction are always available to us. As we grow in our ability to pick up on these cues, we get better at managing each type of personal energy. The checklist below has several clues. Check in with yourself, regularly. Use your responses to build personal energy management efficiency. Build a smooth interaction between expending energy, resting, recovering, and replenishing so that you can begin again.

Personal Energy Leaks, Blocks and Drains Checklist

Please check all that apply	✔
I often feel overwhelmed.	
I usually feel that days are getting shorter and my To-Do List is getting longer. I'm pushing myself to get it all done.	
My thoughts or feelings often wander, making it difficult to be in the moment.	
I'm concerned that my self-care plan (e.g., sleep, exercise, eating well, etc.) is inconsistent or nonexistent.	
Multi-tasking to get things done often leaves me feeling drained.	
My job/career/business demands leave me feeling pressured.	
I get things done in my business/workplace, but I struggle with being creative in my work.	
I'm dissatisfied with my work/family/self/community/play/love/spiritual balance.	
I have way too many emails and projects to manage.	
I have difficulty winding down at bedtime, sleeping, or waking refreshed.	

Too much of the time I feel like Fannie Lou Hamer, "sick and tired of being sick and tired."	
I get stuck in my head thinking and worrying way too much.	
I'm concerned about some goals and dreams that have been on the back burner for way too long.	
My work/career isn't giving me much of a sense of purpose or meaning.	
I struggle with guilt about the balance between time spent on my work/dreams/goals and time spent with my family/loved ones.	
I'm not as confident as I would like to be. I question my decisions and have difficulty moving my goals forward.	
I overanalyze projects and get stuck.	

Physical Energy

We get one body to house and partner with our mind and spirit. She is absolutely committed to us for life. She's unique and specially crafted for our journey. She moves us through each moment. She gives constantly but she also has needs. And trust me, she lets us know exactly what they are because she operates with the highest integrity. In this section, we apply our four strategies--Wisdom, Rhythm, Flexibility and Connection--to the process of building, sustaining and renewing physical energy.

Your body is wise. Get ready to tap into your Body Wisdom. Hone your listening skills. Become an expert at your body's signals for movement, rest, peace, love, food, care. It's all fuel with a guaranteed return on your investment.

Craft a rhythm that keeps your body moving toward wellness and productivity. Use four simple keys to help you get there: Eat, Move, Sleep, and Breathe.

Your body has her ups and downs, ins and outs. Partner with her so that you can adapt accordingly. Build your flexibility muscle.

Your body is your partner. She connects to your mind, spirit, and the world around you. Use this partnership to build, nurture, and fuel her each day.

Body Wisdom

Body Love

I once attended a networking meeting for women entrepreneurs where the presenter, a life coach, took us through a self-development activity. She asked a question that I'd never been asked, but one that I fell in love with right away. "What do you love about your body?"

I was incredibly pleased that a few things came to mind quite easily. Maturity is a blessing. My life experience has yielded lots of gifts, one of which was learning how to fall in love with myself. That includes things that I may want to work on or that I see as a bit flawed.

Anyway, one of my responses was that I like the shape of my body. Even when I have a few more pounds than I like to carry, I still like the shape of my body. Another was the "sixth finger," bump on my pinkie that's just like my father had, only much smaller than his. He was 6'5," and had large hands. My hands and my daddy's hands look like my paternal grandmother's hands. So, they stimulate a deep feeling of connection to my family.

On the surface, this question seems to be directing our attention to physical qualities. But the physical qualities are really a manifestation of something deeper. When we look at our bodies, we see our fathers, mothers, grandmothers, aunties, and lots of others. Even if we're adopted, we seem to take on physical habits and styles of those close to us.

Our bodies are our homes for a lifetime. We won't make it through our lives without them. We need them for everything we do, to make every dream come true, to accomplish every goal, to love, to grow, to experience, to know, to be.

This isn't a secret but it often seems to be one. In his book, *Are You Fully Charged?*, Tom Rath reports a study where his team asked 10,000 people about their energy level the previous day. Only 11% reported that they had a great deal of energy. That's low!

It suggests that most of us are operating below our optimal physical energy level. We're literally running on fumes, if not empty.

Our bodies are suffering and we're ignoring every message they send requesting fuel and recharging. Busy women often stay up late working after everyone has gone to bed, roll out of bed early after hitting the snooze button 18 times or after the third alarm goes off, then rush to manage early morning tasks before stopping at a local coffee shop for a liquid, caffeinated breakfast. They often ignore their growling stomach and simply keep pushing despite fatigue.

If we want to build our businesses, careers, family life, creativity, productivity, and everything that matters most to us, we simply must do better. We cannot live the life we want to live if we don't energize our bodies.

While many people don't change because of startling statistics, most want to be counted among the percent that's reporting a great deal of energy. That group is living the rock star life. They're more likely to be satisfied and fulfilled in each day.

So, where do we start? This will sound very basic, but the first step is to think about how you think about your body. You can't take care of what you don't understand or know. Get in touch with your body.

Some go with the idea that bodies are machines that wear out over time. This group feels they're in a losing battle. No matter what, the body will eventually wear out and there's nothing that can be done to change that. Any improvements will eventually wane and fade away.

Others say the body is a temple for the mind and spirit. This group may feel the body will wear out but they're willing to take some steps to keep it at its optimal level. This group is likely to look for fuel that works as the body's needs change over time.

Physicists would say all matter is made up of tiny atoms supported by unlimited energy that can take any form. Deepak Chopra seems to agree. He says the body is "a field of energy, transformation, and intelligence that is constantly renewing itself."

I agree. Our bodies are pretty smart and they tell us how they really feel. Smart and honest. What better partner could you ask for?

Yes, consider your body your partner in life, one that you can trust. Your body is a wise field of possibility sending you information that will increase your potential. You can build energy when you honor your Body Wisdom.

Take the first step and think about how you think about your body. Are you in the wear out over time, temple, or field of energy group? How do you treat your body as a result of this perspective? Consider how you can begin to shift and see your body's potential and possibility. You don't need to make any big moves. Today, you may be feeling like a machine with a part that needs some repair. For example, you might want to strengthen your arms and create more muscle flexibility. And yes, you might want that tricep dangle to shrink. Tomorrow, you could move toward recognizing that your triceps have the capacity for change with just a little encouragement. With isometric exercises or a few pushups, gentle stretching, time and love, they will transform.

Take the second step and pick some things that you love about your body. Consider why you love them. Do they connect you to your family? Do they ignite your confidence? How and why do these things light up your heart?

Your body has made a lifetime commitment to you. It will signal you, respond to you and go with you everywhere you choose to go. It's your partner and it enjoys being at its best so that it can fully support you. It has senses so it recognizes a range of stimuli, all of which can be used to energize you.

So, let's have some fun using our senses to boost our energy.

Call to Action ~ Use All Your Senses

Pick six ways that you can energize your body. Spread them around your day and week. Make it fun.

Find an energy booster for each one of your senses. Below are a few examples:

> Sight: Look at art or pictures of good memories.
>
> Smell: Try some aromatherapy or take a deep breath in the fresh air.

Hearing: Listen to your favorite music.

Feeling: Take a warm, soothing bath.

Taste: Eat something tasty and healthy.

Movement: Get up and stretch or dance or take a walk a few times a day.

After dinner each day, rate your overall energy level for the day on the following scale: 1 – very little, drained; 2 – low but fine, moving around; 3 – moderate energy; 4 – very good energy; and 5 – a great deal of energy.

Track your energy level for a week or so. When you're on the low end, listen up. Your body is sending a request.

Meet Someone Who Will Never Lie to You ~ Your Body

When an infant cries, people often respond by saying things like, "Check to see if she needs a new diaper." Or "I know you're hungry, baby, your bottle is almost ready." Or "You're sleepy. Let me rock you." We know crying is a baby's way of telling us something is going on. They have needs. We also know that they're listening to their bodies. When their stomach says they're hungry, they let us know. When they're tired, they let us know.

Before we speak any language, we already have the ability to listen to our bodies. Not only can we listen. We can even translate what our body says into crying so that we can get the help we need.

Sometimes as we get older, we stop listening to our bodies. We get tired but we keep pushing. We feel drained, but we don't stop to add more fuel. We feel tension in our shoulders or neck, but we don't stop to relax.

What happens when we don't listen to our bodies? You know the answer. We get sick or injured or so tired that we fall asleep and don't know it until we wake up with our computer in our lap or surrounded by paperwork.

The truth is that our body is one of the most honest communicators we will ever know. If you think of your body as a temple, you know that it's deeply connected to your spirit. If you think of your body as solid matter, you know it's composed of many small particles called atoms. What supports these atoms? Energy, a built-in, invisible and infinite source of power.

Yes. The truth is that our bodies are one of our natural resources. Our bodies feel, move, absorb, and speak. What's one of our best body assets? Our bodies only speak truth.

Let's take a look at some of the common ways that our bodies talk with us. Turn these into a dialogue. Think about how you usually respond and your ideal for being in conversation with your body.

- Pay attention to the little things – I grew up hearing the bible verse, "Your body is a temple for the spirit of God." The body and the spirit have an intimate relationship. They're partners in your life journey.

  Dr. Nan Lu, Qigong Grand Master and Taoist teacher, says that each spirit chooses the body that is perfect for the purpose she came to fulfill. He says, "The body never lies." Aches, pains, tension, butterflies, tingling, gurgling belly, vibrations, all our bodily sensations are information. Our bodies tell us stories about what's happening inside us as well as how we're responding to the world around us.

  Be aware of the range of messages that your body sends you. We've all heard people say, "I think I'm coming down with something." To me, this means they've heard a message from their body. Each of us has to get to know what our aches, pains, tingles, woozies, nausea, vibrations, and other body signals are saying to us.

Take some time each day to check in with your body. Notice the sensations.

What do your signals mean? It may be different, depending on the context. For example, heart rate increase in a meeting with a potential client may not be the same message as heart rate increase while running on a treadmill. Tune in to what your body is saying about what's happening within you and around you.

I invite you to make a game of it. Compare what your body says when you're with your boss versus when you're with your boo. Now this could be challenging if your boss is your boo or you have a crush on your boss. But I think you get the point.

Keep track of this information. Your body talk will tell you when it's time to rest, eat, dance, move away from something, or move toward someone. Get to know your body's language. You will find it useful in making decisions that support your life, health and well-being.

- Get to know how your body's signals for rest and sleep. Resting can be one of the most challenging things for multi-tasking women who do too much. Or women who do it because, "If I don't do it, it doesn't get done."

I know. I'm guilty too. There have been times when my eyes were closing, and I kept pushing myself to stay up a while longer. Not a good idea. The last time that I tried this was the last time I ever tried it. I had no choice but to lie down. My body simply wouldn't go. I'd get dizzy. I was so drained that I had to rest.

In her book *Thrive*, Arianna Huffington talks about being so drained that she collapsed. She treated sleep like it was not a necessity and literally passed out from exhaustion. She was on the floor of her home office, in a pool of blood with a broken cheekbone.

By the time we reach this point, our body has probably been screaming at us. Remember, your body only knows how to express truth. You can trust your body. It is always honest with you. Go to sleep.

- Notice how your body indicates that you are overwhelmed. I've heard people joke, or perhaps they're very serious when they say, "If you want something done, give it to a busy person." Think about it this way. When you have several bags of groceries and you try to carry them all at once, what happens? The bags are very heavy, so you have to stop several times on your way into the house. The bags are weighing you down so your shoulders, back, wrist and/or neck hurts.

Somehow, your body says, “This is too much.” My signal is a pain on the left side of my mid-back. I’ve learned that it’s telling me to stop. I mean really, I stop. I get still. I check in with myself. I recharge. Sometimes I get up and move around. I stretch to relieve my back. I get something warm to drink. Other times I rest. I evaluate what I’m doing. I decide what can wait for another day and what I’ll do after I’ve rested.

- Remember how your body lets you know that it needs fuel. I recently saw an ad for Google where people were asking their phone, “What’s the most important meal of the day?” Breakfast was the answer.

  Throughout the day, our body signals when it needs energy. That could be food or oxygen or other resources. So many times, we ignore hunger or hold our breath. Notice when your body is saying, “Fuel, please.” Have some food. Take a breath. Put energy in so that you can get energy out of your body.

Use these techniques to tap into your Body Wisdom. Build the energy you need to move, dance, skip, run, play, work, and simply be the whole person you came to the world to be.

Call to Action: My Body Talk

Use the chart below to record your Body Wisdom. Notice your bodily sensations and signals for food, rest, emotional distance, relief, sleep, stress management, etc. It may help to choose a few times a day to check in with your body. For example, you could check in on every odd or even hour. Pay attention to what your body says when you have a big project, or you feel under pressure to complete a task.

Indicate how you respond to your body's signals. Do this for a few days. Then look for any patterns. Note the outcome of your responses and consider what, if any, changes you'd like to make.

Situation	Body Talk	Message	Response	Outcome

Body Rhythm

Nap Time and Deep Breaths

When I was a child, up until about second grade, we were required to take naps every day. This was my routine at daycare and at my grandmother's house. Now, while this may have been a tactical way for the adults to take a break or for Mama Louise to get her dinner started, it was an important health decision. My caregivers were strategically placing rest and recovery in my day. Some years ago, I learned that pediatricians recommend children under age 11 get 11 hours of sleep per night. How many of us wouldn't wish for 11 hours of sleep?

Somehow as we grow older, we begin to devalue the necessity of sleep. We can't wait to get to college so that we can stay up and stay out as long as we want. We take tremendous pride in pulling an all-nighter. When I teach about sleep in my beginning psychology classes, I often ask, "How many of you wake up feeling as tired as you were when you went sleep?" More that 50 percent of the students in my 100 – 120 seat classes raise their hands. Most of them are around 18 or 19 years old.

I once reported to my physician that I was having difficulty sleeping. I'd wake up after a few hours and I couldn't get back to sleep. This made for a difficult time getting through the next day. I'd push myself. Work from 8 a.m. until about 7 p.m. Get home. Eat. Attempt to watch television or do some work and what would happen? I'd fall asleep with the computer in my lap or with the television on. When I woke up at 2 a.m. and actually got in the bed, I'd have trouble falling asleep. It became a vicious cycle. And I was exhausted.

When I described my routine to my physician, he said that I wasn't going to sleep. Rather, I was "passing out." Sleep and passing out are not the same, he said. What? I was stunned. No wonder I was having sleep problems. I wasn't going to sleep. He began to instruct me on the importance of a bedtime ritual that allowed my body to get into deep sleep.

As a psychology professor, I don't want to tell you how many times I've taught a class about the different stages of sleep. Our brain waves actually change across the night as we cycle through these stages. In her book, *The Sleep Revolution*, Arianna Huffington reports research about the range of activities that takes place during deep sleep. This stage seems to help us incorporate memories. But important healing work also takes place. Some brain cells shift to allow fluid to flush away proteins that are associated with diseases like Alzheimer's.

Sleep plays a restorative role in our well-being. We rest, and we rebuild. Some psychological research suggests that 7 – 8 hours of sleep per night is associated with better health as we age. We're sharper and better focused when we have good quality sleep. The benefits fill volumes of books. So, why are we fighting sleep?

Somewhere along the way, someone got the idea that working more and sleeping less would give us an edge over our competitors. And some of us decided to over commit ourselves so we actually don't have enough hours in a day to meet the self-imposed demands and sleep.

Here's a major problem, Huffington reports that 24 hours without sleep puts our brain in the same state as someone with a blood alcohol level of .10. We're legally drunk without proper sleep. We wouldn't want an intoxicated person to operate a car, but we will get behind the wheel when we haven't slept properly.

Sleep is not an accessory. It's a necessity. Our bodies don't actually stop during sleep. Our bodies get busy recovering. Cells are restored and renewed. Cleaning and clearing takes place so that we can emerge refreshed.

Similarly, we can use our breath to refresh us throughout our day. When I think back to my childhood, if ever a child cried hysterically, an adult would hold them and encourage them to breathe. They would use their most calming voice and encourage the child to, "catch your breath." This was a lesson on the power of our breath to create calm in our bodies and minds.

Breathing is an automatic function that we can take control of to create a shift in our body. Taking a few deep breaths will transform a stressed state into a calmer one. The heart rate slows. The mind relaxes.

Often because it's so automatic, we forget the many ways that our breath is nurturing us. In *Science of Breath*, Yogi Ramacharaka says, "Life is absolutely dependent upon the act of breathing. Breath is life." All of our body functions depend on our breath. But Yogi Ramacharaka points out that breath can be used to build our mental capacity and spiritual abilities. While advanced yogis learn to use their breath to manage the vital energy flow through their bodies, most of us can benefit from learning simple breathing exercises that help us to restore and recover from stressful times.

Sleeping and breathing, natural functions, are key ingredients in energy management. They're building blocks for replenishing our energy moment-to-moment and day-to-day. In some cultures, businesses close down during the day so that people can rest or take a nap. Some companies, like Google and Huffington Post, have gotten smart about employee wellness. They provide nap rooms where employees can get some shut eye.

Take a look at your sleep habits and patterns. Notice your breathing patterns. Consider what steps you can take to enhance your sleep quality and expand your lung capacity. Take a few deep breaths and close your eyes. Rest well.

You Keep Going and Going and Going – Give Your Body a Break

You know that feeling. You're busy. You're pushing thorough all of your activities. You're taking care of work and family. You may be helping a friend with a project or volunteering at your church.

Maybe your day looks something like this: Be the first person up. Say a prayer. Think about exercising. Maybe do a few jumping jacks. Stretch for 10 seconds. Make breakfast. Get the kids ready. Walk the dog. Feed the cat. Go to work. Get busy. Go to meetings. Feel drained. Try to smile through it. Run errands at lunch. Notice the tension in your neck and shoulders. Answer email. Ignore email. Contact a local business owner for help with the church benefit. Pick up the children. Get home. Make dinner. Feel achy and stiff. Oh no, there's still so much to do!

You have an endless list of things to get done. The more you do, the more the list seems to grow. You keep moving, chipping away at it. Eventually, your body is drained. It's saying, "you have to stop," but your mind is saying, "not yet, there's too much to do."

Even though you may have exercised during the morning or eaten at least one good meal, you're not at your best. You probably skipped at least one meal or picked up something at the nearest vending machine.

What happens? You feel drained, irritated, stressed, blocked, bogged down, or even numb. The weight of your To-Do list is overwhelming. You need energy, but you can't seem to find it.

You're operating in low energy mode. And it feels bad. Your body is responding to your emotional and mental overload. You might even have a few aches and pains. You may be moving slower than you'd like.

Your Body Wisdom is speaking to you. It's not only saying give your body some help now. It's saying, "You need a plan." We have so many demands but very few stops for fuel.

Make this your motto: Self-care. All day. Everyday.

Design a daily rhythm that includes refueling. Stay in tune with your body's needs and signals. Be aware of your body's energy needs. You're busy so you've gotten used to creating routines that make your schedule easier to manage. Put those skills to work and manage your energy throughout the day.

Develop a schedule that allows time for eating, sleeping, resting, breathing, and moving in ways that keep your body healthy. In addition, you can add massage or spa treatments or other health-oriented programs. Once each season I participate in a seven-day program that focuses on eating for healing and Qigong practice. The foods I eat nurture each of my major organ systems at the deepest energy level. And the Qigong stimulates and gets energy flowing around my body.

Look for places in your day where you can stop and refuel. You can start small with 3-5 minute breaks. Tom Rath suggests that you need two minutes break time for every 20 minutes of work time. That's six minutes an hour.

Here are four basics for physical energy:

- Eat for energy and healing – I teach a program based on traditional Chinese medicine, or, as my teacher calls it, medicine according to natural law. Here's one of the most important ideas in this program. Everything in nature has a rhythm, code, or frequency. Certain foods match perfectly with our body systems. Not simply at the vitamin and mineral level but at a deeper "energy," level. I review foods that help to keep energy flowing in our major body systems. Pay attention to how what you eat makes you feel. Does your energy go up or down?

  Nurture your body with food. It can help to make your plate colorful with a variety of veggie selections. Add some red, green, yellow, orange, and purple veggies to your plate. This is a principle based upon the Five Element System used in traditional Chinese medicine. There are numerous book and people resources to help you create a plan that works for you.

  Good eating means making sure you have good food sources available. Vending machines and sugar-filled snacks inviting you to an impulse buy are strategically placed. Be strategic about locating good sources of food.

- Move your body – Movement uses energy but it also generates energy. Some people enjoy the natural chemical boost that can come from vigorous activity or breathing exercises. Others use practices like Tai Chi or Qigong to build the body's vital energy system. Build a collection of activities that boost your energy at every level.

  Here are some possibilities: yoga; breath work; running; walking; swimming; Tai Chi; Qigong; dance; Pilates; or barre method. The list is endless.

  Choose some things that you can do for a quick boost in five minutes or less, like dancing to one of your favorite songs or a short walk or stretching or doing a shimmy and shake for a few minutes to loosen up and relieve stress. If you're really feeling playful, keep a hula hoop handy and give it a whirl.

  Take a look at the list above and choose some activities that you can dedicate 30 minutes to an hour to complete. If your favorites aren't on the list, add them. Be sure that you enjoy every minute. Focus on the activity. Be in it. Notice how your body responds.

  Vary your list of activities. Make sure you include activities that help you build energy reserves for the long haul.

- Rest and recover – You've heard it before. Get enough sleep. The amount of sleep we need may vary from person to person. It may even change at different times in our lives. The most common recommendation is 7-8 hours per night for adults. However, passing out from exhaustion is not the same as going to sleep. When we simply pass out, we're more likely to wake up drained, not rested.

  Develop a bedtime routine. Give yourself an opportunity to slow down 30 minutes to an hour before you go to bed for the night. Let your body know that you're making a transition from active to resting.

  Take breaks during the day. Meditate or sit quietly. Read a few pages of a novel. Enjoy your favorite magazine. Give yourself an opportunity to re-group away from your computer and phone.

- Breathe – Take time to simply breathe throughout your day. For 2-3 minutes or longer, get still and simply breathe. Breathing is a powerful tool for soothing our nervous system in a high-paced world. It also connects us deep within and helps us regain focus. If you're a yogi, try three minutes of alternate nostril breathing. It's particularly helpful during high stress times. Making it a regular practice may encourage less tension throughout your day.

Your body needs fuel, energy. If you're regularly in low power mode, it's time to re-evaluate your energy management practices. Keep your body nurtured so that you can power your life.

Decide what practices work best for you. They may change depending upon your energy needs, demands, resources, or other circumstances. Do what works to keep your body feeling vibrant. Take more naps or go for walks among the trees.

Remember to listen to your body. Carve out time in each day to fuel your body.

Call to Action: Recharge, Replenish, Recover

In the chart below, you will see four essential keys for physical revival and recovery. They are: eat, move, sleep, and breathe. Be sure to spread them around your day but get an early start.

- Start your day with some good food and movement that makes your body feel all kinds of love.
- Throughout the day, take breaks. Stop and breathe.

- If you sit for extended periods, get up and move at 20 – 30-minute intervals.
- At night, slow your body down before getting into bed. This is a great time for breathing exercises, light stretching, Qigong or Tai Chi.
- Most experts recommend 7-8 hours of sleep. Our bodies get their best healing work done in deep sleep, so be sure to give yourself enough time to get there.

Use the chart below and write in the times and places that you will eat, move, sleep and breathe throughout your day.

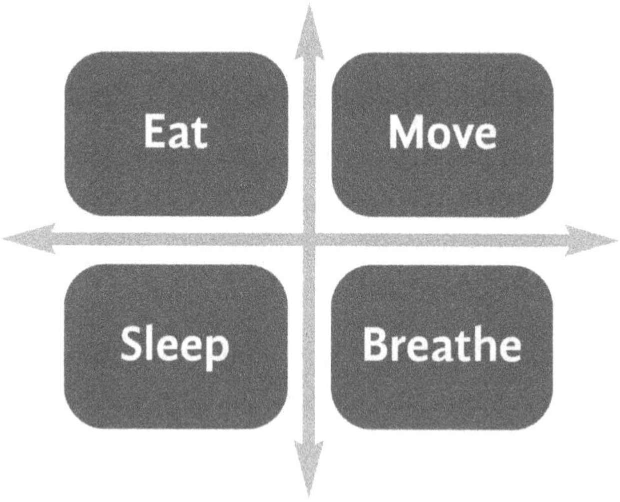

Body Flexibility

Adapt and Find Your Flow

You've heard that phrase, "garbage in, garbage out." It reminds me that everything we do is connected to something and someone else. The way you start your day has a great influence on how you flow throughout the day. Hal Elrod, author of *The Miracle Morning*, says getting a good start is essential for sustained energy as you move through your day.

Everything we do today is a part of building up to the moment we want later today, tomorrow, or simply one minute from now. The physical vitality and health that we want in our future is happening right now. Now is the seed that grows into a forest. Now is the drop in the water that becomes our glorious, resounding waterfall of a healthy life.

This way of thinking is a strategy that we can use every day. Think about it. How do you want your body to feel at the end of the day? What are you doing during your day to get you there? How are you managing your resources? How are you getting what you need to be at your best?

For physical vitality, it's crucial that we monitor our body's cycle. I've heard people say, "I'm a morning person." Or, "I'm a night person." This usually means that they feel more energized, creative, and productive at a certain time of day.

Science indicates that the body has a cycle known as the circadian rhythm. Our blood pressure, breathing rate, heart rate etc. change as the day changes. People who work night shifts have to make adjustments to their sleeping patterns so that they can be awake when most of us are sleeping. It may take some gradual reprogramming of the body so that they aren't constantly fatigued.

In traditional Chinese medicine (TCM), the body has a clock. Each one of the twelve major energy pathways takes a turn being in charge of the body throughout the 24-hour day. TCM practitioners remind us to take note of our patterns. You may notice that your energy level differs throughout the day. You may find that your energy seems to drop about the same time each day. Or you may notice that you awaken at the same time during the night. In TCM, this might be an indication that a particular energy pathway needs some support.

I invite you to note when your energy is highest, lowest, and somewhere in between. Use your knowledge of your energy flow to help you make the most of your resources and determine where to place your replenish and recover activities. Consider what activities demand high, medium, or low energy. Pay attention to the activities that seem to boost your energy and those that seem to drain it. Make the most of your flow by scheduling activities to coincide with your level of energy when possible. This will help you adapt and develop flexibility

For example, I'm up between 5 and 6 a.m. doing my morning routine. So, I aim to get to bed by 10 p.m., 11 p.m. at the latest. I like to use my early mornings for creative writing projects. After my morning charge-up routine, my mind is fresh and my body feels good. I'm deeply connected to my spirit. I find that my posture and breathing are easy but strong. My ideas seem to flow more easily as I sit comfortably and confidently. Most people would consider me a morning person.

However, as we know, there are times when we're called to expend more energy than we may feel is available. Like that meeting scheduled at 3 p.m. when all you really want to do is sit quietly or take a nap. During these times, it's important to be intentional about giving your body an energy boost.

Before the meeting, stop and breathe. Or get up and dance. Take a walk. Have a good snack, or some combination of things that gives your body the boost it needs. You can also consider rearranging your schedule on days that you need to attend a meeting at 3 p.m. Perhaps scheduling low demand activities in the few hours before your meeting will help you preserve some energy for later in the day.

When your body is refreshed, you have more resources available to complete tasks. Be flexible. You can test out different strategies to discover which ones work best for you. Have fun discovering what works for you and when and where it works best for you.

Call to Action – Take Me Up, Take Me Down

Use the form below to record your physical energy levels across the course of the day. Rate yourself on a scale of 1-10 with one being little to no energy and 10 being very high energy. You can think of each number as a percent. 1 = 10%, 2 = 20% and so on up to 10 = 100% capacity. You can choose 4 – 6 times each day to check in and record your rating.

Time	Rating	Situation

Make recordings for at least five days. Note any patterns such as an energy drop at certain times of day or during certain situations. When you notice a decrease in energy at the same time each day, no matter what you're doing, use this as a signal. Consider adding an energy booster or relaxation activity before this time of day.

If you find that certain activities leave you, "zapped," then consider how you will adapt. Is this an activity that you need to continue doing? If no, then you can delete this from your life? If yes, then consider these questions. Is this a necessity that someone else could take care of for you? Perhaps this is an activity that you can delegate to someone in your support system. If it can't be delegated, is there a way that you can do it differently? Perhaps changing the timing or your thinking about it would increase your energy to get it done.

Body Connection

Love Your Body and It Loves You Right Back

Do you ever have those days when you dread going to the gym or taking a walk or getting to yoga or practicing Qigong? You know that you'll feel energized after your workout but, "Ugh!"

Perhaps you're like me and right in the middle of a class you say something like this to yourself. "What was I thinking? Why didn't I take the day off? Oh no! Seat work. What, lift my leg up?" You want to escape but you know that you can't. You gotta go through the experience.

My guess is that afterwards the chances of feeling vital, refreshed, and ready are above 90%. Throughout the day, we might notice we're more willing to take stairs or we sit up straighter or we're calmer or more focused. We may be more in tune with our body's request for food or water or rest.

We are likely to notice changes in our physique or the way our clothing fits. We might look younger or more rejuvenated. People may ask us what we're doing. Or inquire what kind of skincare products we're using. They may even say, "you don't age."

There are definite benefits to turning ugh into oomph. Our bodies are quite responsive to self-care. There's a nice feedback loop between our investment and our outcomes. We put energy in and we get energy out. And of course, as we witness the fruits of our energy output, we're inspired to do more.

Researcher Albert Bandura created a psychological term for this, "reciprocal determinism." He noted that the interaction between our environment, behavior, and personal factors like thoughts and personality determined our future actions. Bandura believed that we impact our environment and our environment impacts us.

For example, you enjoy yoga and like to practice regularly. There's a studio near you that you frequent. You may take advantage of special offers or package deals so that you get an opportunity to practice often. After classes, you notice the peace of mind and increased ease in your body. You may also like the convenience or the instructors or the cleanliness of the studio. Both the physical reward and your thoughts about your experience and your environment leave you wanting more.

The studio owners may notice that classes have higher attendance at certain times of the day. This may lead them to offer more classes at these times. When they get a good response to packages, they may offer more options for clients. They may also offer other services like mat rental or childcare to support customers. The more responsive they are to your personal needs, the more you may want to practice at a particular studio. The more you and other clients practice there, the more the owners are likely to grow and enhance services.

In this case everybody is winning. Your body, mind, and spirit are winning. Your host studio is winning. Your community is winning with a thriving business.

Numerous factors connect and interact to make you a winner at physical revival. On those days when you're feeling a little like ugh, use this to your advantage. Get started by creating a feedback loop for 1 – 3 of your favorite ways to love your body.

Take a look at the diagram below.

1. Begin by choosing an activity that you use to love your body. That's your "Behavior." Let's say that you enjoy Tai Chi. Record you answer in the "Behavior" circle.
2. Think about where in your, "Environment," you like to do this activity.
    a. This could be a room in your home with nice lighting or beautiful plants, a quiet space.

   b. It could be a park or a local business.
   c. How does this environment support your behavior?
      i. Record your answer in the "Environment" circle.
   d. How does your behavior support the environment?
      i. Record you answer over the bi-directional arrow between "Behavior" and "Environment."
      ii. For example, if you practice in your home, you may be motivated to keep the space ready and peaceful for your practice.
3. Think about the benefits of your behavior. Really get into thinking about what you love about the activity. Go deep into your body's positive responses. Don't skip the little discomforts that may arise. Even mildly sore muscles after a workout remind us that our bodies are benefitting from our activity. It says, "Congrats! You grew. You changed. You got a little more today."
   a. Record them in consequences.
4. Notice the thoughts you have about your behavior and its consequences as well as the environment where you practice.

a. How do your thoughts support consistency in your activity?
b. What do you say to yourself after your practice?
c. Record these in the "Thoughts" circle.
d. Make sure that some of these thoughts are positive comments and congratulations to you for taking care of you.

Make this a fun activity. Maybe you'll get really excited and turn it into a vision board for your physical revival. Whatever you do, remember to "Rock it!"

Call to Action: Creating a Win for Our Bodies

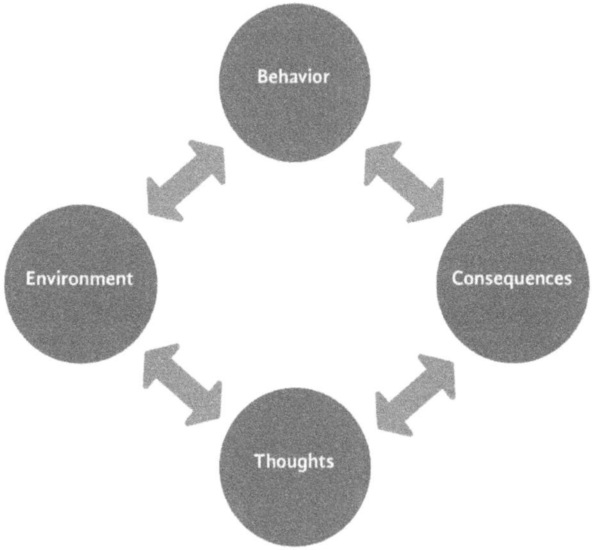

Person to Person ~ The Power of Human Interaction

The cure of a person is another person.
~ Wolof Proverb

The things that we most treasure, like fairness or kindness, require action. We have to translate them into our behavior. We want to behave in a way that makes it most likely that the good things we share with others will come back to us. I remember talking with a colleague who's involved in social justice work in schools. We talked about how often scholars take action in a community where they work but fail to translate their philosophies into collegial relationships. They're busy saving the world but neglecting the people right in front of them. As a child who grew up in the Atlanta, Georgia, this is in direct contrast to my southern roots. We learned that you speak to and extend kindness to everyone.

I saw a video of a morning activity in a classroom for small children. They sat in a circle. The activity begins when two children place their hands in prayer position, bow to each other, and then hug each other. One child in the pair then turns to the next child and passes on the bow and hug. They continue until everyone in the circle has greeted the person next to them with a bow and a hug.

Imagine that. Start your day with acknowledgment and love from others. The school day, like the workday, occupies a significant part of our life. How wonderful to start it off with love and honor from those who spend the day with you.

This is one reason that the Wolof of Senegal in western Africa say, "The cure of a person is another person." If a family member has to be hospitalized, another family member accompanies them. People are not left alone in the business of healing. But we don't need a major illness in order to support another person. You can probably remember a time when another person did something nice for you or simply said, "Good morning," and your whole day shifted in a better direction. It's one of the things I love about traveling to southern states. People, random people, perfect strangers speak to you. They even ask how you're doing. And they smile.

These basic human decencies can be quite powerful when we are open to receive them. They remind us that we matter. That we are not alone. That others recognize our value. These experiences are good energy boosters.

In *Are You Fully Charged?* Rath reports his team of researchers found that people who had more positive interactions throughout the day reported higher levels of well-being. Yep, smiling, holding a door, and paying someone a compliment all make a difference in our daily well-being.

These brief exchanges show us the power of human connections. It's reciprocal determinism on steroids, creating an endless ripple effect. Someone gives you a smile. You feel a boost in energy. You're more productive. You call a client and your voice sounds like a big smile. The client engages and benefits from your service. They spread the word about your work. Your business grows. And you're smiling and sharing your joy with others.

Positive interactions are gifts that keep on giving. Rath says that if we want to be fully charged, they are an essential ingredient. You need them for your personal energy management plan. Good things do come in small packages. Most of these kindnesses can be completed in 10 seconds or less. Random acts of kindness can have a lasting impact. You give, and people pay it forward in their interactions with others.

If you're having a bad day or bad interaction, consider a small step you can take to begin turning things around. Consider how you could be more positive, giving, or understanding. Perhaps, it's better to table a conversation and make a promise to come back to it once you've given it some thought. Perhaps the other person has a good point and you can simply take a moment to look for the good in their perspective.

Pay close attention to your behavior. Notice your body language when you're interacting. Be present in your exchanges with others. Early in my career, I provided psychotherapy to adolescents. Yes, you guessed it. Many of them had no desire to be sitting in an office talking about problems they didn't believe they had. Sometimes, the best way that I could make a connection with them was to notice their breathing pattern. I'd start by matching their pattern. Then, I'd notice what I was feeling. What was my breath telling me? Anger? Fear? Uncertainty? I let my body connection lead me to a question. Sometimes teens weren't clear on their parents' concerns or they were angry that their parents couldn't see their point. So, this is where my question would start. What do you think your parents are worried about? Why do you think your parents are concerned about you?

This became our beginning. We could build once we had a connection. Your goal is to experience and create positivity in your relationships. You want to build relationships that have the power to sustain you and those around you.

Create as many small positive interactions as you can throughout your day. This may mean you'll need to pay less attention to your phone when you're with others. Yes, you guessed it. Research shows that people rate interactions as more productive and more positive when cell phones are not visible. In a 2014 study, The iPhone Effect, Misra and colleagues examined 100 dyads and surveyed participants about the level of empathy they felt from their conversation partner. People reported higher levels of empathy from their partner when mobile devices were not present. This effect was consistent despite effects related to age, ethnicity, mood, or gender.

What's the takeaway? Be with the people in front of you. Allow your interactions to power you up. Be present so that you can return the favor for your partner.

Call to Action ~ Share Good Stuff

- Develop a list of strategies for creating positive interactions.
- Practice random acts of kindness.
- Be sure to notice the kindness that you receive from others. Savor the good feelings and energy pump that you get from someone's thoughtfulness.
- Be mindful about your mobile devices and leave them out of your conversations.
- Notice the impact on your physical energy.

Physical Energy Chart

Physical Energy Recharge, Renew, Replenish	
Body Wisdom	Listen to what your body is telling you. It always tells the truth.
Body Rhythm	Design a daily self-care plan to nurture and restore your body.
Body Flexibility	Adapt your routine to maximize energy resources.
Body Connection	Allow the gifts of self-care to motivate you to be consistent.

RECOVER YOUR BODY MIND SPIRIT

Mental Energy

As a yoga teacher and a psychologist, I've learned volumes about our mind. The short and not so simple version is that our mind includes our thoughts and emotions. Many of us have heard the phrase, "Get your mind right." We know the mind, while invisible has a powerful impact on our day-to-day life. We transform what's out there in the world or even what's happening in our bodies into something that makes sense to us. In this section, we apply our four strategies-- Wisdom, Rhythm, Flexibility and Connection--to the process of building, sustaining and renewing mental energy.

Tap into the seemingly infinite capacity of your mind. Everything begins with a thought. Learn to use your thoughts to tap into the power of your deeply held beliefs. Build the mental energy you need for forward movement.

Organize your thoughts into words that guide your actions. Use your internal dialogue to create a steady rhythm, a march toward your goals.

Learn to shift your attention. Be flexible in your assessments. Reframe your experiences. Get the most out of every life experience. Use your thoughts to recognize how everything advances you.

Learn the power of clearing your mind. Do nothing in order to get something. Stoke your creativity. Notice how creativity supports productivity and vice versa. Use the connection between your thoughts and actions to power your focus, decision-making, and problem-solving.

Mental Wisdom

Mind Your Head

Speak what you seek until you see
what you said.
~ Anonymous

Growing up, my Mama's regular biblical guidance was, "As a man thinks so is he," and "Be ye transformed by the renewing of your mind." Her goal was to rear spiritually grounded children clear about the power of God within and around them. Not only did she do that, but she also gave me the secret to creating my best life.

Actually, it's not really a secret, like something you try to hide. It's the magic kind of secret, like an ingredient that makes all the difference in your outcome. You may remember Mike Dooley from the video, *The Secret.* He became well-known for saying, "Thoughts become things."

There's a seamless connection between our thoughts and what we do. Let's say you're hungry or you need to choose an outfit. Before you eat or put on your clothes, you'll see the food and clothes in your mind's eye. Even if you get dressed in a rush, you had to think about the outfit before you put it on.

Shakti Gawain's *Creative Visualization* was one of the first spiritually oriented books that I read on mindset. She wrote about a spiritual law, namely that form follows thought. Your ideas, your thoughts, the images that you hold in your mind are your blueprints. From a spiritual perspective, they guide the energy to flow into form in our physical world.

There is great consensus on the power of our thoughts. The bible, Taoism, physics and so many other traditions, philosophies, and epistemologies (just a fancy way of saying this is how we figure things out) agree about this idea. It's natural order. Before we see it in physical form, we think it. Once you think a thing, it's real, no matter whether or not you can see it right away.

At a physical level, thoughts are invisible frequency patterns created from neural activity in our brain. At a metaphysical level, thoughts create vibrations in our everyday experience. I know you've seen this happen. You're thinking about someone and they call. Or you need a red scarf and a friend calls and says, "I've got something for you," then shows up with a red scarf. Or you meet someone who develops websites when you need one for your business.

In cognitive behavioral theory, the thoughts in our immediate awareness are sometimes referred to as our automatic thoughts or internal dialogue. But they're based on a deeper system. At the deepest level of our mind, our beliefs are running the show. They're inner guidebooks for our lives. They are templates determining our every move.

Beliefs function like little waffle irons pressing out our mental conversations and our feelings and our behaviors. Some folks make square waffles. Others make round ones. Still others make waffles that look like Mickey Mouse. This analogy makes it easy to see how changing your waffle iron can change your life. New beliefs = new you.

Here's an example from my experience as an entrepreneur. I spend time in workshops, masterminds, webinars, books, and conversations with other entrepreneurs learning and putting strategies into action. I'm transforming the picture of my business that lives in my head and heart into the picture that I see in my life every day. It often seems that there's some magic involved in growing a business. I want to make my invisible thoughts appear in my everyday life.

Yeah, I know building a business requires work. You have to put your nose to the grindstone as some say. You have to invest sweat equity. You need a plan. You have to take action on your plan.

Not only do you need a plan, you need a vision. You need to visualize and feel what's it's like to be a leader in your industry. You have to know what your client will have after they've purchased your product or service.

So, quiet as it's kept, you have to be a bit of a fortuneteller. If you sell coffee, how do you present it in such a way that your customer feels uplifted and so yummy that not only do they come back, they invite friends and they give gift cards for your coffee as presents to people they really love.

If you're a coach, how do you partner with someone so they realize they have everything they need to accomplish their goals? What do you do to get someone to realize that they are the power that makes their life the one they really love living?

And once you know your audience and what problem you can help them solve, you have to figure out how to speak to them so they realize that you're on the same page. You have to attract them.

And the last time I checked, when people are attracted to something or someone, there's some soul stirring, magical, "yes that's so right for me," stuff going on inside them. Like so many songs say, something just "feels so right."

But you can't see attraction. You don't see the magnetic waves making contact with your customer and drawing them in. However, when they show up excited or wait in line for days at an Apple store to get the latest iPhone, you know a connection was made.

On some level, building my business depends on very powerful invisible forces like vision and attraction. That's probably not as magical as it might seem at first. It's pretty simple--everything begins with a thought.

Since thoughts are based on deeper beliefs, one of the most powerful things we can do is to get really clear about our beliefs. We have to know the beliefs that support our goals and the ones that keep us from our goals.

Why? Because sometimes we have competing beliefs. That is, we give ourselves mixed messages. This creates what my Mama calls the, "I didn't know If I was coming or going" effect.

For example, let's say that you are looking to sign a new client or implement a new project or start a new wellness program. Part of you is saying, "Yes, this is great. Go for the contract, it's a good deal." Or, 'Yes, this is the perfect project. You'll make a major impact in your industry." Or, "Girl, you are gonna look and feel so good. Your body is going to be the poster child for health." However, at the same time there's a competing voice saying, "That's too big of a contract. You can't make that happen." Or, "Who do you think you are? You can't handle that much attention." Or, "You know you're not going to keep that up. You love brownies. No way you're gonna give them up."

Are you coming or going?

Jim Rohn says, "Your income is determined by your personal philosophy." He says it's the guidance system of our mind that helps us minimize dangers and maximize opportunities. We do things based on what we "know." Our beliefs are what we know. They become thoughts and actions or inaction.

So, "mind your head." Just like my tall dad often had to bend a little when entering a room, it's important to monitor our thoughts. Overthinking, excessive worry, and rumination are energy drains. My college students will tell you that overthinking is why they choose the wrong answers on exams. Remember, some of those times when you spent too long thinking about starting a project or purchasing an item. By the time you got around to it, the people who could partner with you had moved on or the product sold out.

Yes, of course, you will start right where you are and move forward from there. When one door closes, another one opens. But notice when you're going down the road that holds you back from your dreams, what's important for you to manifest in your everyday life. Is there a thought that has become a broken record in your head, stuck on repeat? Pay attention to what the worry is telling you. This is known as self-monitoring. Once you name it and listen to its guidance, you can set a plan to problem solve or prevent issues.

Truth is, our beliefs and thoughts are energy sources. They get things moving. They can motivate us toward our dreams. We have to decide to choose the beliefs that move us closer and closer to our best life. Our mental abilities are one of our greatest resources. Use them wisely.

Call to Action ~ What Did I Say to Me?

1. Get to know your thoughts. Choose a thought that you consider troublesome and track the times that it shows up in your experience.
2. The words in your head may be slightly different each time, but you know it's basically the same thought.

3. For example, you may find that you don't ask for help when you need it because of thoughts like this: "I don't want to be a burden. People don't have time to assist me. They have their own stuff to take care of."
4. After recording the thought, record how you responded to the situation.
5. Finally, record any consequences that you notice. Record what you notice in yourself as well as what you interpret in others' reactions.

Situation	Internal Dialogue	Response	Consequences

6. Once you have several different situations, look for themes.
7. Then consider what belief is underneath these thoughts. What kind of waffle iron are you using to press out these thoughts?
    a. It may help if you question the thought that's coming to mind. For example, if you're saying you don't want to be a burden, ask yourself why? Maybe you'd say it's

not fair. Then ask again, why isn't it fair? You may answer, I'd be taking away time they need for themselves. Eventually, you may realize you have a belief that you don't deserve help or that you have to be strong and do everything on your own. You may uncover a belief that people won't extend love toward you.

Mental Rhythm

Put Your Mouth on It

Women in my grandmother's generation often used the phrase, "Don't put your mouth on it." They were not referring to something that should not be ingested. This was their reminder of the power of the spoken word. To "put your mouth on," something is to give it the power to manifest. It's a highly valued and time-honored idea in various traditions around the world.

In the Dogon cosmology, Nommo is associated with this power. The ancient African mother deities Yemonja and Auset are said to be the mouth of power and to have the ability create by the power of the mouth. Even the symbols chosen to represent the ancient African language, Mdw Ntr (commonly called hieroglyphics), indicate that words have divine power. In English, Mdw Ntr translates to word of God/The Creator/The Oneness. And of course, there are the well-known mantras associated with Hindu tradition, often used in meditation to foster greater connection with the divine and the divine power within us.

In our everyday lives, we may be more familiar with phrases that athletes use to help them focus and use their abilities to the fullest. Or we may have read about the powers of positive thinking or taken a stress management class where we developed positive self-statements to assist us with remaining calm under pressure. What's even better is that many of us have discovered that positive self-statements can help us access the inner resources that we need to accomplish a goal.

Various researchers have uncovered data that supports the traditional ideas—words have power to help us create change. Dr. Candace Pert even demonstrated that our thoughts are transformed into chemical messengers that match the emotion associated with that thought.

Words reflect our beliefs but at the same time words can become beliefs. Thus, affirmations are both a goal and the foundation for achieving a goal. When we create an affirmation and use it, we begin to see ways that we can develop a skill or gain a new perspective on a challenging situation.

We can use the power of our words, especially what we say to ourselves to impact our daily experience. We all have goals such as: Lose weight. Get a new job. Mend a friendship. Get fit. Reduce stress. Be more patient. Start a business. Write a book. Build a house. Start a hobby. Take a vacation. Make a bucket list. Volunteer.

What's in your heart? What do you really, really want right now? What makes it important to you? How will it make you feel?

Loved. Joyful. Excited. Vibrant. Satisfied. Free. Peaceful. Fulfilled. Safe. Confident. Courageous. Focused. Decisive. Clear-headed. Proud. Energized.

I think of goal-setting as a roadmap. When I was growing up, my mother kept a map in our car. If she hit traffic or thought there might be an easier way to her destination, she would pull over into a parking lot, take out the map and plot another course.

Since I was the oldest, I often got to co-pilot. She'd show me the route and I'd help navigate. We got out of a lot of traffic jams and found some shortcuts this way.

But what it gave me was a sense of personal power. I learned that I could find my way around any obstacle or make my journey easier. I could find a way to keep moving, keep flowing.

Setting goals does the same thing for us. It's a plan to help us get where we're going and move around, over and through our challenges. When we set goals and follow through, we use the power of order. We get into our rhythm.

We can identify exactly what we need. We can plan how big of a step to take and when we need to recharge so that we can keep moving.

We find things to look forward to and get excited about. We can even put in some resources, like support networks, so that we have enough energy to get us through the rough times.

What we say to ourselves is one of our most valuable and potent resources. We can develop positive self-statements or affirmations to help us connect to a concept and draw on the way it impacts us. If we set a goal to be more peaceful, we can simply begin by stating that we are peaceful. As we repeat the word, it stimulates images and emotions and actions associated with peacefulness. Our nervous system responds. We begin noticing what peaceful feels like, tastes like, smells like, sounds like, and looks like. These affirmations become our tools for building our best self.

It's an excellent practice to begin at any time. You can design your affirmations to focus on a goal that you want to achieve, to set the tone for your day, to create a mood, to cultivate a skill or even as stimulants for an emotional state. There are numerous possibilities to reap the dividends that come from investing in a few well-chosen words.

Affirmations help us link words to actions and emotions. They provide a means for understanding how our beliefs are the foundations of our actions. We see that growth is intimately tied to the ideas in our hearts and minds. Words become seeds that grow and manifest in our reality. We give our words and our most sincere intention then we harvest the marvelous returns.

Using the power of our words can be a very rewarding practice. At the beginning of each year, you can choose three words that will guide your year. Develop them into affirmations to say each morning throughout the year. For a few years, I chose love as one of my words for the year. The other two words were usually related to my personal development or other goals.

Love, ease, and satisfaction is one of my favorite combinations. The affirmations include:

- I walk through my day attracting and expressing love, ease, and satisfaction.
- I am love.
- Ease and satisfaction are in every moment.

Using affirmations encourages me to look forward to good experiences. In fact, my Taoist teacher, Dr. Nan Lu, says a key to having what we want in our lives is to "change your beliefs about your future." He says to believe that whatever happens in your future is for your good.

This is a message that I've heard from other spiritual teachers. My mother sent me a message from a minister that she follows. It said, "God is already in the future working things out for your betterment." Another spiritual teacher, Esther-Abraham Hicks, recommends meditating on the phrase, "Things are always working out for me."

Ask yourself, "Do I believe my future holds only good for me?" If you cannot reply with a resounding, "Yes. Absolutely," it may be that you've been so focused on doing, pushing yourself, and taking the steps toward your goals that you forgot the big picture. Many of us move through life at a fast pace. We've got vision boards and lists of goals. Our eyes are set on the prizes that we want in our future. When we're in hot pursuit of a goal, it's easy to lose sight of the deeper benefits, the why behind our goals. The end game isn't things, it is peace, freedom, joy, autonomy, growth, fulfillment, compassion, wellness, or other sources of internal reward.

It may also be true that you're giving yourself two messages. At the same time that you're reciting your affirmation, "I am peaceful," you may be giving yourself a counter-message. The other dialogue in your head might be, "There's no way that I can be peaceful with all these responsibilities." Or, "Yeah. Sure. I'll be peaceful the minute somebody else is doing all this work." If you feel that your affirmations are falling flat, check in with yourself. There may be some beliefs you need to acknowledge and move through to elevate yourself.

Affirmations about our future can ignite our optimism and help us stay focused on the deeper benefits of our accomplishments. These are the everlasting goodies. They're not visible to the naked eye but the emotional and mental power they awaken can't be measured. They set our soul aglow.

When you think about it, the next moment is the future. Your affirmations can help you experience the good in the next moment and the one after that and the next one and so on. Allow yourself to truly experience your affirmations. Use all of your senses. Get every last drop.

Go ahead. Put your mouth on it.

Call to Action: Words of Power

Here are some tips on using the power of words:

1. Think about your goal. Decide what you want.
2. Create a statement that indicates you already have it. Be sure this statement reflects what you want rather that what you don't want. Thus, if you're trying to reduce fear, put your intention on being courageous or confident or secure or self-assured rather than fearless. Think about what you'll have when there is less fear. What is it that you want?
3. If you're aiming to accomplish a goal like weight loss, think about how you'll feel when you've lost the weight. Then, create affirmations to help you claim those feelings.

Here's an example. Perhaps you work in a very stressful setting. You sometimes find yourself feeling anxious, moving fast but not getting much done. You'd like to be calmer, more centered, peaceful, focused or all of the above.

- If you're new to affirmations, choose one word and create a sentence such as, "I am calm," or, "I am focused."

- If you're more experienced, try combining two words such as: "I am peaceful and focused."
- Be patient with yourself. Take some deep breaths and say your affirmation. Repeat it regularly. Notice how your behavior begins to match your words and your words remind you of the feeling and behaviors that make the words your reality.

Call to Action: Eye Openers ~ Good Start

- Who's the first person to know that you're awake? You. So, who's the first person you greet in the morning? You. Take the first two minutes of your day and greet you. Say something positive to you. Remind yourself that you're connected to a wonderful web of energy or God or the Universe or loving people. Remind yourself of who you are and that you're on an important, indispensable mission.
- You've just learned a strategy for creating affirmations. In the latter part of the book, you'll give your purpose a name (if you don't already have one). For now, come up with a short statement that you'll say to yourself in the first two minutes of your day. You're simply going to take some deep breaths and repeat it to yourself before getting out of bed.

- Here are some examples
  - I am a spiritual being having a human experience. Today, I look forward to fulfilling my mission as a child of God/The Creator/The Universe.
  - I am a child of God/The Creator/The Universe. The world is a better place because I'm here. Today is an opportunity to share my good with the world.

Call to Action: Make Mental Magic

- Get your day started with some affirmations, then use the power of what you say to yourself throughout your day.
- It's perfectly wonderful to say them at different points throughout the day. Consider including them in your nighttime routine too.
- One of the most powerful ways to use them is for stress reduction. Dr. Donald Michenbaum created a strategy known as Stress Inoculation Training (SIT). Psychotherapists have had great success using it with a range of experiences. We can use the guiding principles of SIT to help us manage everyday stressful situations.

- When you're anticipating a challenge, think about what you will say to keep yourself centered:
    - Leading up to the situation
        - ★ Include statements that remind you that you're ready or prepared.
    - During the situation
        - ★ Include statements that remind you of your goal and get you back on track when you feel distracted or lost.
    - If you become anxious during the situation
        - ★ Include statements that help you refocus and bring you back to your goal.
    - At the end of the situation
        - ★ Include statements that acknowledge your accomplishments.
    - After the situation is complete
        - ★ Note what you did well as well as how you learned from this experience. Consider how this experience will help you improve.

Mental Flexibility

Blessings in Disguise ~ Transform Failure into Progress

When I was a child my mother used to say, "It's a blessing in disguise." During my younger years, I never really questioned this idea. Somewhere inside me, I chalked it up to my mother's optimism, her unyielding faith that God is on her side. Hence, all is and will be well. As a young person, I made a sincere effort to see the blessing underneath the disguise. After all disguises weren't too bad. Wearing a costume or mask on Halloween was a way to get candy and other goodies. So, surely a blessing in a disguise might be even better than one that showed up in plain clothes.

However, as I grew older, I also grew intolerant of this process. I wanted my blessings to show themselves clearly, to stand up and say, "Over here," or "Here I am. I've been looking for you." I became uninterested in disguises and even less interested in trying to find the blessing underneath them. I found the disguises were sometimes quite complex. I mean, where could the good possibly be in not getting a promotion when I wanted it or a failed relationship?

My mother, however, persisted. "Just look at it as a blessing in disguise," she continued to offer. It didn't matter whether or not I told her about my disappointments, I could still hear her voice in my head. Sometimes, she would quote the bible, "All things work together for the good of those who love the lord.," Yet, I often struggled with the idea that difficulties could be a part of building my greater good. Unfortunately, this meant my focus shifted from looking for the good to staring at the bad.

I've heard numerous spiritual teachers and practitioners say, it's universal law that whatever we focus on grows bigger. My mother knew this too. She was not encouraging me to be Pollyannaish or ignore challenges. Rather, she was nurturing my ability to use spiritual science--the ability to use my mind and spirit to cultivate good within and around me. She was gently guiding me to move beyond the surface and get beneath my experiences.

We know there will be ups and downs. We will have successes and failures.

Just like when we were children, we will learn to deal with the wins and losses. Most of us find it easy to embrace success. This means we're a winner.

Failure, on the other hand, is not always so easy. We get stuck in our minds going over where we went wrong. We get worried about falling behind, not being able to take the next step in our business or career. We start comparing ourselves to others and chastising ourselves for not being as successful as someone else.

Our mental and emotional energy take a downward spiral. And we are headed to rock bottom. There's great momentum but we're moving in the wrong direction.

Is there an experience that you'd like to see differently? Is it possible that you've overlooked a gift while staring at an empty space? Perhaps you've managed to get to a better place about a loss or a disappointment and as you look back on it, you can see the gift you received. Can you see that the bid that fell through on the first house you wanted led you to a better deal and a home you adore? Did the union in your workplace negotiate a better contract after you were denied your first promotion, so you got a bigger raise when you succeeded on the second try? Just take a moment to notice.

There are gifts awaiting you. You only need to shift your focus. Remember, what you focus on grows bigger. Grow your good.

> *"Helped are those who find something in Creation to admire each and every hour. Their days will overflow with beauty and the darkest dungeon will offer gifts."*
> *~ Alice Walker*

Call to Action ~ Grow Your Good

1. Think of a situation that you seem to only see in a negative way. Perhaps you're experiencing difficulties and most of your thoughts are about what's going wrong. In fact, you focus on what's wrong, though there are probably many things that have gone right. You may feel overburdened by the things that you dislike.
2. Try this each time you hear the tape recorder in your head that's stuck on a repeating negative message. Examples include:
   a. "My relationship with ________ is growing more peaceful every day."
   b. "I have all the resources that I need to accomplish my goals."
   c. "Everything I need is available to me."
3. The statement should reflect what you want to cultivate. Be sure to repeat it several times. Breathe into it. Imagine what it looks like, feels like, tastes like. Use all your senses.
4. You'll have to be mindful that you don't go back to your old script. This sometimes happens when we feel overburdened. If this happens, remind yourself that good is your inheritance, your birthright. This is a non-negotiable truth. Think of the good you want and attract it to yourself.

Call to Action ~ Four Steps to Transform Failure into Progress

Complete this worksheet using the steps described below.

What's Your Why? • How does this project fit into your bigger picture?	
Reframe • What went wrong? • What did you say to yourself? • How can your internal dialogue help you improve?	
Be flexible • How can you get back on track? • How can you improve your timeline?	

Be thankful • What are your blessings in disguise? • What did you gain from this "fail forward?"	

1. Remember to keep your name ~ Huh? Yes. Remember to keep your name. When things don't go well, we often change our name to "failure." We focus on our inadequacies and these become our definition of self.

   Take a moment and be nice to you. Experiencing a failure does not mean that you are a failure. Reconnect with your why, your purpose.

   In truth, the project that went wrong is a part of a bigger plan. The project adds meaning to your life and provides you with a means to make a contribution to your family, community, and even to the world.

   Having meaning, purpose, and making a contribution are the wins that you're working to get. Put your eyes on the bigger prize.

2. Reframe the meaning failure ~ Remind yourself that this is an opportunity to make your

project better. You can improve it, enhance it, or take it up a notch.

Sara Blakely, Spanx Founder and CEO, provides a great reframe of failure. She says her father had a regular practice of asking her what she failed at. He would high five her when she tried something and failed. He expressed disappointment if she didn't fail at anything. This meant that she didn't try; she didn't make an effort to accomplish a goal.

Blakely came to understand not trying as the tragedy rather than trying and failing. It reminds me of that saying, "Nothing beats a failure but a try."

To get your mind in order, write down all the things you're saying to yourself about where you went wrong and what you should have done. Now use this list to develop a problem-solving strategy.

Remember, thoughts and feelings are clues. The thoughts about your errors are guidelines to order your plan for progress.

3. Be flexible ~ Sometimes we need a side step in order to move forward. Give yourself some options. There may be other avenues to achieve your goals.

Check out how you're using your resources. Do you need help with this project? Do you need more time? Sometimes the goal is so clear to us that we rush toward it but may not give ourselves sufficient time to achieve it.

Add some flexibility to your timeline. Give yourself some wiggle room. Giving yourself a time range (e.g. – 4-6 weeks) to complete a project may help you manage and direct your resources to get it all done.

4. Be thankful ~ I've heard the phrase, "Fail fast, fail early, and fail often." I don't know who said it first but when I hear it, I think, "Failure is a good thing, something to be thankful for."

   Be thankful for the opportunity to improve and grow. Be thankful for the opportunity to find a little more of the best in you.

   One of the things I love about yoga is a little progress makes a great impact. The first time you try to stretch, you may meet some resistance. But you simply look for the slightest possible bit of room. A miniscule amount is acceptable and feels good.

   Failing opens the door to discover a little more of the greatness in us. When we use it to progress and share our greatness with others, we create a win-win.

Take a moment and write down what the failure helped you discover about yourself. Be thankful for the gifts.

A Mission for Self-doubt – The Impostor Detective

Every year I look forward to celebrating my birthday. My Taoist teacher helped me expand my practice of honoring the day that I entered the world. He encourages us to use the energy of our birthday as a catalyst to move our personal development forward.

Various traditions honor the power of our birthday. Many African traditions say it marks the moment our spirit chose to come from the ancestral realm into the physical world. Astrologers talk about the Sun returning to the place it was at the moment you were born. These ideas affirm our connection to our genetic heritage and the very universe where we live. Thus, the invisible energy surrounding our birthday is like a colossal, solar-powered jetpack that we can use to accelerate progress on our personal vision.

One year, in addition to my personal and business goals, I chose to focus on facing a personal challenge specifically, self-doubt. You know, those thoughts that make you wonder, "Can I really do this?" They seem to show up when you get moving on a project.

I call self-doubt the "Impostor Detective." It reminds me of a skilled professional, like EZ Rawlings or Sherlock Holmes or Tamara Hayle, truly talented at collecting the necessary information to verify that I'm masquerading and can't get the job done. I sometimes imagine that it's dressed in a trench coat using a magnifying glass on my inadequacies.

Self-doubt can stop you right in your tracks. Instead of moving forward, you start thinking of all the reasons you should stop or why someone else would be better at it or how much better it would be if and when you had such and such or how it's too late or that someone else is already doing that so why would anybody listen to what you have to say anyway.

The list of reasons why not to move on goals can be long and winding. It can wrap right around us and keep us stuck, idling or even backsliding. It's very easy to see self-doubt as the evil, sneaky enemy, out to thwart our plans.

But how about we flip the script. Change up. Take a new look at self-doubt. Find the beauty in the beast. Or as the poem says, look for the silver tint in the clouds of doubt. That's a perfect balance, a perfect complement. It's a definitive expression of flexibility.

When I decided to make that birthday year one where I explored my self-doubt, I said, "I don't want to make it an enemy." As the natural order would have it, we come pre-installed with our own security system. Doubt, fear, worry, or any thought or emotion that gives us pause is like a little alarm or traffic sign pointing us to something that needs our attention. I made a commitment to pay attention rather than get a big stick and try to beat back the big furry thing puffing at me.

I chose to put my reframing skills to work. But this meant I had to sit with each situation. I had to invite the Impostor Detective for a chat. One thing about detectives is that they collect information. They're inquisitive. They look for patterns. They connect one thing to another.

My job was to figure out what connections were giving my self-doubt a boost. What was the basis for the conclusion that something wouldn't go well? What was the supporting evidence? Was there any evidence to the contrary that could be considered?

My Taoist teacher says that everything is moving us to our greatest expression of self. He and my mother believe that everything happens for our good. Luckily, during the months prior to this birthday, I made an active effort to look for good in all of my challenging experiences. So I was primed to go deeper and make some changes.

Jonathan Fields wrote a book titled *Uncertainty: Turning Fear and Doubt into Fuel for Brilliance*. The title alone inspires. It says that you can be scared and brilliant. Being afraid can unlock the door to magnificence. Maybe he knows my Mama and my Taoist teacher.

Early in the book Fields writes, "Anything certain has already been done." That's like, if you always do what you always did, you'll always get what you've always gotten. Or same s#$*, different day.

And of course, there's the quote:

> *"If your dreams don't scare you, they're not big enough."*

The first time I read this quote, I felt both rewarded and challenged. I had a, "Yay, I'm dreaming big because I'm scared as hell," and an "Oh, no, this doesn't stop as long as I keep dreaming of doing and being more of my best self." Either way, there's no getting around it. I'm going to be working with, around and through fears, doubts and other nagging thoughts and emotions.

Brilliance requires disequilibrium. Uncertainty is certain when you're going for your dreams. Fear, doubts, and taking risks can energize us toward impressive outcomes. They stir us up. We can use them to grow, get our plan in order and execute it.

By the end of my year making friends with my self-doubt, my courage and confidence grew. I moved a research project forward. I completed some writing projects and I had some difficult conversations. I stood up for myself in situations where I might have "just let it go," and failed to acknowledge my skills or contributions. By the next year at our birthday meeting, I announced my new goal: Be my bold, badass self. The second year, I announced my goal: Be my bold, bad ass self with ease. No pushing, but acting with certainty that I can and will fulfill my divine purpose. I will make a meaningful contribution to uplifting humanity and social good in our world. And I will do it with peace of mind, full of faith, and satisfaction with my path.

The Yoruba sacred text Oshe Meji says that lack of faith or self-confidence is a tragedy. Why? Because it contradicts the sacrifices and investments we've made to overcome our difficulties. It suggests our successes aren't meaningful; that what we think we cannot do holds greater significance than what we've accomplished. But most of all self-doubt can disconnect us from the power of our purpose. We're here because we can do what we came to do.

Call to Action ~ Sit Down with the "Impostor Detective"

By now you know that if we want to get unstuck, we need to uncover our automatic thoughts and the beliefs that generate them. This is a five-action process for turning self-doubt into the engine that propels us and puts wind under our wings rather than the one that grinds us to a halt.

You'll need to set aside some time to review the experience where the Impostor Detective showed up. In the moment, you may need to create a pause for yourself. You might say, "I'll get back to you." Or, "Let me give that some thought." You'll want to make some quick notes in your diary or whatever smart phone app you're using to track important information. Maybe you'll send yourself an email with some details about the situation. Then later commit to a sit down with the Impostor Detective.

The more you practice this process, the more prepared you'll be. You'll unearth the beliefs that need your attention. You'll find evidence of your abilities and you'll get more and more comfortable with being your "bold, badass self," with ease because everyone of us is the best.

1. Acknowledgment
    a. Notice what you feel. Fear. Doubt. Uncertainty. Anxiety. Confusion. Inadequacy. Skepticism. Hesitation.
    b. What's the situation? Who was there? What transpired before you felt doubtful?
    c. Pay attention to your bodily sensations and what you're saying to yourself in that situation.
    d. Trying to ignore these feelings and thoughts will likely intensify them. Why? Because our thoughts and emotions are our security system. They're pre-installed. They're warning lights that say, "Fix this so you don't have a bigger issue."
2. Assess
    a. Determine what issues the feeling is trying to get you to notice. Be clear about what concerns you in each situation.
    b. Here are some questions to consider.
        i. Are you afraid that you don't have a necessary skill? Do you doubt your abilities?
        ii. Are you concerned about being overwhelmed, lack of financial or physical

resources to complete a particular task?

iii. Is there some person that you need to contact to be successful?

iv. Do you need support or an accountability partner?

v. Are you overthinking your plan and getting stuck in resistance? Has procrastination become your constant companion?

3. Reframe criticism

 a. There will be typos, grammatical errors, and other things that are a bit out of place. Feedback about these things will only help us be more brilliant. Revisions make things better.

 b. Yes, there are mean people who may criticize simply to be mean. That's what they need to do. It's not a statement about your worth or the significance of your dreams.

 c. Decide how you will use every experience to turn up your light. Ask yourself, "What good can I get out of this? How will this help me grow?" Transform the situation into personal growth. Identify what your thoughts and feelings of self-doubt can teach you about your strengths and character.

d. Look for successes you've had in similar situations. Remind yourself that all the resources you need to fulfill your purpose are available to you.

e. Treat everything as information to help you get better. Use whatever shows up in your experience to move you forward.

4. Problem Solve

    a. Make a plan to resolve your concerns. Then, use it to help you keep building your dream or moving toward a goal. Define and secure needed resources. This could be people who can help or skills you need to develop.

    b. If you need a skill, then research books, courses, and people who can help you. Next, go for it. Go to class. Get mentored. Read. Do what you need to turn off the warning light and reset your system.

    c. Recognize that there will always be some risks. You'll have to take them. Seth Godin says, "If you wait until you're ready, it's almost certainly too late." The subtitle of Patricia Ryan Madson's book, *Improv*

Wisdom, is *Don't Prepare, Just Show Up*. These ideas remind us that our dreams are worth the risks. The world needs what only we can bring. Trust you.

d. Look for the beliefs that are running the show. What patterns are showing up in your automatic thoughts? Have you come to believe that you don't deserve to succeed, you're not good enough, things don't work out for you, people will always be mean to you, failure is bad, failure means you're inadequate, or other beliefs that maintain self-doubt?

   i. Locate your first memory associated with this belief. When do you think that you locked in on the idea? What happened that led you here?

   ii. Now locate information that doesn't support this belief. For example, if you think you're not good enough, look for accomplishments. Amass some evidence that you are "good enough," and begin to shift your mindset so that setbacks don't turn into "self-bullying."

5. Positive Self-Talk

   a. Develop some affirmations and coping statements. We can be good at saying mean things to ourselves like, "How could you make such a stupid mistake?" Or, "You're so naïve." Or, "Why won't you stand up for yourself?" Or...okay, you get the picture. There's no need to bully you.

b. Use your self-talk to get you to a better place. You can use these statements when you feel overwhelmed by an experience or as you work through the situation that gave rise to your self-doubt. Here are some examples:
   i. "I can use my anxiety to help me. Let me focus on what it's showing me."
   ii. "Okay, I'm nervous, take a breath. Focus. I can figure out the best step to take right now."
   iii. "Everything happens for good. Let me locate the gift in this experience."
   iv. "I am growing more confident."
   v. "I am patient with myself."
   vi. "I prepared for this. I trust myself."

You can use this worksheet to help you apply this five-action process.

Sit Down with the Impostor Detective	
Here's what happened:	
Acknowledgment	
Assess	
Problem Solve	
Reframe	
Positive Self-Talk	

Options, Opt-in, Optimistic

When in the midst of sorrow
You can't see up when looking down
A brighter day tomorrow will bring
~Sounds of Blackness - Optimistic Lyrics

We often remark that time is flying. The day is gone. The year is half over. What have I accomplished? After many years of spending time with teachers who use the seasons to guide their wellness practices, I developed a new awareness. Mother Nature is a great planner. I live in the northern hemisphere. So, when the second half of the year arrives just as summer begins, many of us slow down, regroup, and indulge in some luscious pleasures. Beach day. Spa day. Vacation. Mountain cabin. Lake. Here I come.

The summer arrives right at the time we're wondering where the time has gone. We're taking stock and looking at where we've been and where we are. Our New Year's resolutions may be thoughts that flew away with the year, but we're very likely evaluating whether we're still heading toward our goals. As we look back at our goals and resolutions, we're very likely to rate ourselves. We've got plenty of information to help us figure out what went as planned and what may have taken a detour.

The good thing is that nature is working right along with us. We have more room in our lives to take inventory and revise plans. Some things have probably gone off track, but the warm and sunny outside can make us feel warm and sunny inside. The flowers are bright and pretty. Nature is showing us what it means to flourish. The earth, plants, wind, water, and minerals have been in a dance for several months. They've been mixing energies and chemistries to produce summer fruits and flowers.

For Nature, there may have been a few extra cold days or a little less rain or some other obstacle, but she kept pursuing her goal. So, no matter what may have gone off track, she delivers her goodies when summer arrives. She gives us the best she has each season. She fits everything into her plan to make it all work together.

The ability to move around over or through obstacles is an essential aspect of optimism. The optimist sees possibility. They're often said to be the people who look at a 16-ounce glass with 8 ounces of water and say that the glass is half full. Pessimists, on the other hand, would say the glass is half empty. The pessimist doesn't simply notice what's missing. They see what's missing as an indication of limited possibility. They see it as a predictor of low chances of success. The optimist will look at what they have, work with what they have, and figure out how they can grow it into what they want. Their gratitude for what's there helps them open to more. They're receptive.

Early in his career, psychologist, Martin Seligman developed the learned helplessness theory. His work showed that people in difficult circumstances will often remain there even when there's an opportunity to escape those circumstances. Their early efforts to escape met with failure or were ineffective so they simply stopped trying. They stopped believing that they could create change. Seligman's work contributed to our understanding of depression and other challenges to our well-being.

However, he continued to ask critical questions about the connection between our thoughts and our behavior. He's recognized for his leadership in developing the field of Positive Psychology. He moved from studying pessimism to studying optimism. Great move! In his book, *Authentic Happiness,* he points to some key differences between these two approaches to making assessments and choices.

According to Seligman, when things go wrong, pessimists believe the events are permanent. The bad condition will always affect them. Bad events will always happen. Optimists think these events are temporary. Things could change in their favor and they can take an action that creates that change.

When things are going well, optimists think good experiences have permanent causes. There's a strategy or resource that they can use. Thus, optimists believe that they can repeat good experiences over and over. Pessimists see good events as temporary, the result of luck or unexplainable causes. For the pessimist, their actions don't have an impact that brings good into their lives.

Optimists, like my Mama says, believe that "Trouble don't last always." There's a way to a better place.

Even if the glass is half empty, there's a faucet, a water fountain, a store that sells bottled water, a resource that they can tap.

In actuality, many of us have been optimistic in some situations but pessimistic in others. What would you say is your most frequent pattern? Is your glass half empty or half full? If you're in the "half full" group, then you're reaping some benefits that come with optimism. Productivity, decreased likelihood of depression when confronting difficult times, and better stress management are among the goodies.

If you're in the "half empty" group, no worries. Seligman's research shows us that optimism can be learned. Yes. We can build mental and emotional flexibility. We can shift the way we look at things. We can get a new pair of glasses. We can build and flex our optimism muscles.

Perhaps, you don't think you fit easily in to either category. You see the glass as half full and half empty. You're looking at the whole picture. You see what's missing and the possibility of improvement. Yep. You fit in the optimist group.

Strengthening your optimism muscles builds mental and emotional energy. When you feel as though your energy is waning, check in. How are you judging the glass in front of you? Wherever you are right now is the perfect place to start. Redirect your energies. Advance your goals.

Seligman offers some guidance that I translated into an optimism workout.

Call to Action ~ Build Your Optimism Muscles

- Name it
  - When you have a pessimistic thought, take a look at the situation. What occurred just before your thought? Name what's happening.
- Notice your thoughts
  - What's going on in your head? Identify the beliefs that support your pessimistic thoughts.
- Feel what's happening
  - What are the emotional consequences of your thoughts and beliefs? How do the pessimistic thoughts and beliefs leave you feeling?
- Be flexible
  - Now ask yourself if there's another way to understand what's going on. What are some other ways of looking at the situation? Can you find any positive aspects of the experience you're having?

- Claim the relief
    - Mental flexibility and finding positives in our experience relieve tension. We can see other possibilities. We have the energy to move forward with optimism.

Name It • Describe the situation. What got you here?	
Notice Your Thoughts • What's your internal dialogue?	
Feel It • Describe your emotions.	
Be Flexible • Look for alternative explanations. What's the good in this situation?	
Claim the Relief • Describe the energy boost and relief.	

Analysis Paralysis ~ Get Out of the Corner

When we're working on something that's really, really, really important to us, it's easy to get caught up in what went wrong or what will go wrong. We look for what's missing, where we fell short the last time we tried this or where we might fall short the next time. I once watched a television show where a character talked about his brother's unwillingness to do anything that he thought would end in failure. The brother would go over and over the potential for failure in his mind. If it seemed something might go wrong, he'd keep analyzing it trying to figure out where the missteps might occur.

Evaluating a situation in an attempt to create the best outcome is a good thing. Why? This supports efficiency in our actions. We develop plans that work when we consider odds, pros and cons, and other details. We can make the most of our resources.

However, it becomes challenging when we only notice what's not right, what went wrong or what might go wrong. This thought pattern often ends in disappointment, questioning our goals, indecision, and feeling drained.

The process is referred to as "analysis paralysis." We need to make a decision or craft a plan to move a goal forward. We want something. But we're not moving because we're overthinking.

The desire for everything to be perfect is one of the easiest roads to analysis paralysis. It's an impossible endeavor to leave no room for criticism, to get it absolutely right on the first try. The effort to consider every possible thing that might go wrong and attend to every detail is futile.

In analysis paralysis, our thinking is out of balance. We've got too much focus on could'a, would'a, and should'a or what if. Eventually, our mental energy is blocked. Indecisiveness has us stuck. We've got lots of ideas and no action. We no longer see that the missteps could be a source of energy that propels us forward.

We need to alter our course. Balanced mental energy requires that we are flexible so that we can make the most of our thought resources. Analyzing every tree has its place, but we also need to step back and look at the forest. When we reach a dead end, we need to look for open road.

Rosetta Thurman of Happy Black Woman offers a very simple directive: "Start now. Improve later." Lisa Nichols of Motivating the Masses says, Leap with your imperfection and make it better as you are soaring. Nike says, Just do it.

When we're stuck in our heads, it's time to look for where we can make a move. That's the power of balance. This principle teaches us how to use complementary forces. It's like that toy, the slinky. It was a metal coil. You held one end in each hand and gently nudged it so that the coil would easy move back and forth between you left and right hand. Finding that sweet spot in the middle of left and right creates movement.

Movement is the partner to being stuck. They are complementary forces. Thus, when we're not moving, we look for a way to make even the smallest movement. Let me confess, I've been in the perfectionist circle many times, so I've developed some skills at getting unstuck. I start with small steps and give myself deadlines. Then, I get friends to take a look at my first steps and give me feedback. I use what I learn to get better and more comfortable in my head. As I get more comfortable, I can take the next step.

I remember something that my elders often say, "You get another chance. Each time you get better." Heck, the message on my answering machine even says, "Make every day better than the day before." Just a little change can make a big difference. This is one of the reasons that I love yoga. You feel a little stiff. You may not be able to move three inches, but maybe you can move a half an inch. Move a half an inch today;

another tomorrow and the next day and so on until you're at that place you want to be.

Remember, when you're stuck, move something.

Call to Action ~ Make A Move

Noticing the next smallest step we can take is a movement toward getting unstuck. Make a list of things you can do to get moving when you're stuck in your head.

- What gets you started?
- How can you make the slightest move and shift your thoughts into forward gear?
- And don't forget to check out what program you're running in your head. What beliefs are underneath your perfectionist, analysis paralysis thoughts?

Mental Connection

Do Nothing to Get Something

I am a human being, not a human doing. Don't equate your self-worth with how well you do things in life. You aren't what you do. If you are what you do, then when you don't...you aren't. ~ Dr. Wayne Dyer

I've heard so many people say that they cannot meditate because they cannot slow down their mind. They say each time they try to get quiet, their thoughts start racing. They're doing one thing and then another in their heads. One name for this constant chatter is monkey mind.

Sadly, our attempts to meditate aren't the only time our minds shifts gears in rapid fire. Consider those times when you're in a meeting or at lunch with a friend or at your child's school play. Rather than being present in the moment, your mind is on other things. Or you're constantly checking your phone while you're at an event or a meal with friends.

Some of us can't sit still for very long. The statistic often quoted is that our attention span is shorter than that of a goldfish. I mean, really, that's about five seconds. After that we're on to the next thing. Reading an article or a newspaper is out of the question. It would take way too long. We'd have to slow down.

The result is that you're not present. You miss the experience you're in. You can't enjoy the moment because your mind is elsewhere. And sometimes, you've even moved your body to another space, picked up your cell phone, or fired up your computer.

First, let's settle this question. Does the mind have to be completely empty when we meditate? Um. No. In an interview with Krista Tippet of On Being, Matthieu Ricard, Buddhist Monk with tens of thousands of mediation hours, shares that he spent many of those hours distracted. He encourages us to think of meditation as mind training. You're training your mind to focus. Distraction is part of the process.

The movement in our mind leads us to seek focus. We can start small. Over time our ability to focus grows. What happens next? Interestingly, the more we're able to focus, the more ideas begin to flow, easily and logically. A reasonable solution to a problem may come to mind. You might begin to see how all the pieces fit together.

Rather than a jumble of ideas moving all over the place, we get a story that makes sense. Our mind is moving but there's a deep sense of ease or comfort. When we reach this place, we've tapped our inner knowing. We accessed a deeper level of our consciousness. It's that place where we connect the dots in our experience and we see how our experience connects to others.

One of the most delightful aspects of this place is that we crave more "mind quiet," time. It's a great cycle. Monkey mind leads us to quiet our mind, which creates a flow of ideas, which makes us crave more meditation. Now, when the monkey mind shows up, we realize it's the beginning of the journey to flow of ideas.

Less doing and more being is essential to mental harmony. One of my favorite quotations is from my Taoist Qigong Master.

"Doing nothing is doing something."
~ Dr. Nan Lu

It was a strategy he offered for creating more peace of mind and harmony in our daily lives. Many people say that you can't get something out of nothing. But in this case, yes you can.

It's pretty easy to see how this works. This is one small way that we can begin to quiet our monkey mind. Simply stop. Sit still. Close your eyes. And take three really deep breaths. Keep your eyes closed for about 20 – 30 seconds, less if you're a descendant of a goldfish.

When I do this, I feel relaxed and focused. Right away my body and mind benefit. And the only thing I've really done is what I do all day – breathe. No big moves here. Just breathing. We do it all day, but in the hustle and bustle, most of us think of it as nothing.

Doing nothing is a powerful way to get something. It reminds us that we can use complementary forces to enhance our well-being. When our minds are cluttered or scattered, it's an opportunity to define focus and peace of mind.

As we explore what we don't want, we get better at defining what we do want. The contrast between where we are and where we want to be helps us to create a roadmap to get us there.

Below are some of the best "do nothing" strategies. There is a ton of research on the benefits of meditation and deep breathing. These practices enhance our nervous system. Our genetic structure even changes in ways that are associated with increased life expectancy. Basically, meditation can help us fix ourselves up.

Digital detox is also getting well-deserved praise. In *Are You Fully Charged?*, Tom Rath tells us that people are more productive and have better interactions in meetings where cell phones are not visible. Disconnecting from your phone and computer opens room for you to move out of the reactionary mode. Rather than constantly responding, you can get your juices flowing and be proactive.

So, power down your phone, take a deep breath, and focus on you. Power off so that you can power up.

Call to Action ~ Power Down to Power Up

These do-nothing strategies can help us create a change of pace. Unplug so that you can plug in to your true power source.

1. Meditate ~ Take a few minutes and focus inward. Three deep breaths will usually slow you down. Then choose a statement that allows you to keep your mind still. It can be an affirmation, a Sanskrit mantra, a bible verse, or a favorite quote. You choose. Remember the statement should be one that helps you reconnect with and maintain that "umm good," flow feeling. If you're short on time and you don't have 10-15 minutes, take 5, 6 or 7 two-minute breaks throughout your day. That's easy

enough. You can take two minutes when you go to the bathroom or to get a cup of tea.

Thich Nhat Hahn, Zen Buddhist Monk, teaches a tea meditation. The goal is to be fully present with your cup of tea. Begin by simply noticing the smell of the tea. Sip slowly and notice the flavors in the tea. Hahn teaches a form of mindful meditation. He says that the essence of meditation is living in the here and now. Every moment in your life is a meditation.

Thus, we always have an opportunity to meditate. Hahn conducts walking meditation. He's even done them on the streets of New York City to demonstrate that no matter where you are, you can find peace. In an interview with Oprah, he described the process. As you breathe in, take two steps and say to yourself, "I have arrived. I have arrived in the here and now in order to touch the wonders of the world." As you exhale, take two steps, saying, "I'm home, home, home. My home is in the here and now." Hahn teaches that being in the present moments helps us to release the regrets about our past and worry about our future.

2. Practice Qigong ~ Qigong is another technique for quieting the mind, stimulating the body's

restorative abilities, and centering in our true source. It's a system of movements and standing postures based on the five-element system, ancient science defined in traditional Chinese medicine. Elements like fire, water, and earth correspond to energy systems in our body like heart, kidney, and stomach. Each element also has an emotional and spiritual component and corresponds to an energy network that extends throughout our body. My Taoist, Qigong Grand Master calls this our "inner-net."

Free flow of energy keeps the body, mind, and spirit balanced and working in harmony with each other. Qigong movements and postures are created to nurture the subtle flow of vital energy through our body's energy system. For those who have difficulty sitting or finding stillness while sitting, a standing Qigong meditation posture could be an alternative. While the postures appear simple, they offer significant benefits and are often accompanied by a deep feeling of peacefulness.

At a physical level, subtle shifts in energy encourage the body to balance and heal. A healthy energy system helps us to process our emotional experiences. At a spiritual level, the gentle movements or standing postures connect us to the infinite source of energy that sustains life within and around us. A Qigong Master can teach you the science and spirit of this self-healing technique. Many have developed DVDs and CDs to educate and guide you through the practice. A few reported benefits of Qigong include decreased anxiety and stress, better sleep, improved digestion, improved health, and greater peace of mind.

3. Breathe ~ Yes. Breathe. There are so many breathing techniques that help us slow down, tune in and power up. One of my favorites is alternate nostril breathing. This one calms my anxiety in three minutes. Three minutes!!! If you've ever taken a yoga class, you're probably familiar with its miraculous benefits. You can also take 10 deep breaths. Deep breathing pairs well with meditation. In fact, focusing on your breath is one of the easy ways to develop your meditation muscle. Each time your mind wanders, come back to focusing on your breath. Inhale. Exhale.
4. Digital Detox ~ Disconnect from your cell phone, email, Twitter, Facebook, social media, computer, all of your digital connections for a few minutes each day. Start with 15 minutes and then increase the amount of time as you become more comfortable. Perhaps, you can

work up to lunch without your phone or any digital connections. Have lunch with a good friend or colleague and turn off your phone.

Go on vacation and put your cell phone and computer away. Enjoy nature. Take in a museum. Read a book, a paper book. Give yourself a break from the constant barrage of digital signals.

Create and Produce ~ The Power of Continuity

Blue cows. Purple unicorns. Red squares. Yellow hearts. What? You're very likely wondering about these combinations of colors and objects.

When you read those words, images came to mind. The same thing would happen if I told you, don't think of blue cows. Don't think of purple unicorns. Don't think of red squares. Or don't think of yellow hearts. You're still getting the same images.

That's how easily our thoughts work. Think it and instantly you can see it, feel it, and know it based on your experience. It's true cause-effect. Have a thought and see its effect. It's an example of reciprocity in action.

Our imagination and creativity are among the most powerful tools on our energy belt. Creativity and imagination are both a cause and an effect of performance and productivity.

Remember a time when you felt most creative at your work. Perhaps when you were just beginning a project, your business, or designing a costume for your child's upcoming party, you had ideas and visions that really got you moving. You chose colors and elements for your logo that captured the spirit of your business. You designed products and services that spoke to your clients' needs and deepest desires. You thought about the atmosphere that you wanted to create. You thought about how your project would impact your audience. You imagined how your child would look and feel in their costume.

Sometimes while making breakfast or sipping a cup of tea, you got a big idea. You wrote it down, maybe on scraps of paper. You began to see it, know it as the reality of your work.

I call these "juicy times." Our mental energy is glowing and flowing. We've got ideas and images. We're writing and developing programs and creating websites and building networks and serving clients and nurturing happiness in those we love. Our creativity increases our productivity.

And here's the cool thing about reciprocity. Our productivity is a stimulus for creativity. We might create a program that gets praise from a client. Their positive response as well as their wishes for how it could be better gets our juices flowing. We see how to improve the service, take it to the next level, and make it even better for our clients.

Or we're working on an idea and the more we develop it, the clearer it gets. We begin to see the stages for growth. We see how to progress our ideas.

Creativity and productivity work as a team. They nurture each other in a way that increases our mental energy. This intimate connection encourages us to focus on the ways that our projects speak to us. Rather than simply doing things to get them done, we begin to notice what we're getting from the project, how it's a catalyst for our growth and self-expression. We can use our productivity to stimulate our creativity and vice versa.

During times when we're feeling unproductive, we can get creative to stimulate movement. We can use the partnership between creativity and productivity to increase our mental energy.

Call to Action ~ Get Excited

Here's an easy way to design "juicy times." Recall some creative experiences. What got your juices flowing? Were you around a certain group of people? Did you see something while on a walk? Were you doing one of your hobbies? Were you looking at the clear blue sky on a sunny day?

Your goal is to find those things that stimulate your creativity. It can help to use all of your senses. Think of things that you see, hear, taste, smell, feel, or ways you move that stimulate creativity.

You can also remember projects that you developed in your most creative state. What did you produce? How did it impact you? Remember, use all of your senses.

Mental Energy Chart

Mental Energy Recharge, Renew, Replenish	
Mental Wisdom	Be mindful of your thoughts. Notice what program you're running.
Mental Rhythm	Minimize distractions to maximize clarity.
Mental Flexibility	Embrace the power of reframing your perspective.
Mental Connection	Build your focus muscle to find your mental flow.

RECOVER YOUR BODY MIND SPIRIT

Emotional Energy

Emotions can be thought of as a personal GPS (global positioning system). They're intimately tied to our thoughts and actions. If something feels right, it's a go. If not, we're hesitant. Emotions add value and richness to our everyday experience. They're available to energize our passion and help us craft our caution into the next step in our personal evolution. In this section, we apply our four strategies--Wisdom, Rhythm, Flexibility and Connection--to the process of building, sustaining and renewing emotional energy.

Uncover the messages in your emotional experiences. Explore the partnership between your thoughts and emotions. Learn to use the power of your emotional wisdom to power your goals and life vision.

Listen to your emotions. Identify your stress signs and symptoms and how to use them to get the most out of your experiences. Claim the emotional experience that you crave. Let your emotions guide you to a new, more productive rhythm.

Use your emotions as a guide for personal expansion. Explore shifts that create flexibility in your comfort zone. Identify strategies that enhance your emotional intelligence. Become more mindful of the freedom that comes with monitoring and making gentle shifts in your emotions.

Apply simple strategies for making the most of gratitude. Connect to the good in your life and elevate your feelings of thankfulness. Reveal the power of this simple action to energize your body, mind and spirit as well as your relationship with the people and the world around you.

Emotional Wisdom

Emotions Are Taking Me Over

I know I'm dating myself, but I can hear that Bee Gees song. How did the words go? Something like, "It's just emotion taking me over. Caught up in sorrow. Lost in this song." Or as some would say, you're wallowing or drowning in emotion.

There are times when our emotions seem overwhelming, out of our control. Uncontrollable. Unmanageable. It may even seem that the more we try to control our feelings, the more intense they become. Or perhaps the more someone says, don't be afraid or nervous or worried, the more you feel that way.

I'm reminded of a workshop I attended some years ago. The presenter talked about dreams and how they're interpreted across cultures. She told the story of a South American culture where people are taught to face fears that show up in their dreams and to look for the gift their fears have to offer. Consider this, a child awakens and tells her parent that she was frightened because she dreamed that she was falling. The parent might respond with, "Next time, be sure to look and see where you land." Or if the child dreamed a large, scary animal was chasing her, the parent might advise her, "Next time, stop and turn around to see what gift the animal had to offer you."

I know. Sometimes we'd rather simply run away from something scary. It's hard to imagine that the scary thing has anything worthwhile to offer us. But remember our earlier discussion about self-doubt. Your fears, like your doubts and worries, are signals to stop and solve a problem. Imagine them as arrows pointing you toward clues that can help you resolve an issue. So, your worry that a client won't like your proposal may be an invitation to review your proposal and address the points that may be of concern. Your fears about trying a new sport may be reminding you to make sure you take the necessary safety measures or purchase the equipment that will support your physical well-being.

I remember working at a summer camp. The children were full of energy. Some could do cartwheels and hand stands. Others couldn't. Those who couldn't do these physical feats kept trying until most of them were doing cartwheel drills around the outer boundary of our meeting room.

One girl would occasionally make a minimal effort, but you could see the fear in her face from a mile away. When we sat and talked, she shared how scary it was to try a cartwheel or handstand. I asked what did she fear might happen. She was afraid that she might fall on her head.

It's a reasonable fear. Falling on your head is definitely dangerous with possible long-term consequences. I agreed this was possible and invited her to think of this fear as an arrow pointing to an issue with some solutions. The issue was how to protect her head while trying something new. She could practice on a thick gym mat. She could have one of her parents spot her while she practiced. She could practice handstands on a thick mat pushed against the wall so that the wall would stop her. She could first practice what it felt like to place her hands down and hop up a foot or so. As she got more comfortable, she could jump higher. In addition, she had lots of role models that she could watch to learn their techniques.

So, what's your cartwheel? What thing leaves you afraid that something will go wrong? Perhaps, you're avoiding a difficult conversation with a supervisor or supervisee. Maybe you're doing someone else's job and concerned about what might happen to your relationship if you stop covering for them. Perhaps, you really need a break but people are looking for you to lead the way and you're afraid of letting everyone down. You may have a book you want to write or a business you want to start or a piece of artwork that's been developing in your heart and mind. But you have yet to take that step because, "What if it fails? Miserably?"

Our emotions are our built-in traffic signals. They say, "Stop. Look over here. Pay attention to this. Watch out. I've got something to show you. Take care of this before you move forward." Yes, emotions, like thoughts, are our personal security system. We've all probably had our car or house alarm send out a signal. Despite the deafening sounds and the tense startle they create, we're glad for the warning. It gives us notice that something unwanted is underway but "you've got time to fix it."

So, at the same time you may be frightened, you're called to action. You can get focused and clear about what steps to take. In that moment when the alarm is blaring, you can locate your calm in the center of the storm and map out your actions. Your affirmations and positive self-talk guide you through the moment. Stay focused. Get to safety. Call for assistance. You're grateful for the warning and opportunity to take action.

I like Thich Nhat Hahn's analogy for emotional challenges. He says it's like a mother whose baby is crying. She cuddles the baby gently and soothes the baby. Hahn says our pain, our anxiety, is our baby. He says to recognize and embrace the suffering. Use your awareness of the suffering to get to the root, to understand the nature of your feelings. In doing so, you will see how to transform and free yourself from it. The difficulty becomes the way to a better place.

There are times when our emotional response to a situation stops us in our tracks. We can't move toward a goal because of fear of something we think might happen. Our anxiety about things we "can't quite put our finger on," keeps us stalling or stuck.

How can we use this signal, this "crying baby," to get moving toward our goal? Below are some actions you can take to use your emotional wisdom. Your emotions are showing up for a reason. They're one of your partners in life. Listen to what they're telling you. Learn to negotiate and use these signals. As Hahn suggests, the more our awareness grows, the shorter the time we spend suffering. We grow in our ability to transform our difficulty with greater ease.

Call to Action ~ My Emotional Alarm System

1. You will want to set aside some time to review the situations where your fear, anxiety, or other troublesome emotion shows up. Try to complete this activity as close to the time of your emotional experience as possible. If you don't take the time right away, be sure to make some notes about your experience. Use the chart below to assist you.
2. Describe the situation. Who's there? What did they say? How did you respond to them?
3. What emotion were you feeling?
   a. Give it a name.
   b. Note any bodily sensations that you experienced.
4. What did you say to yourself? What was your internal dialogue?
   a. Remember these thoughts will help you locate the beliefs that are driving your mental and emotional experiences
5. Identify the unwanted thing that your emotion is pointing out for you. What is the problem that needs your attention?
6. Identify some action steps that you will take to address the issue.

a. Some action steps may be short term while others may be longer term actions.
b. What small thing can you do in the immediate future to address the concern that's coming up for you? It may simply be that you to take some deep breaths, center yourself, and get clear about your goals.

Situation	Emotional Response	Internal Dialogue	What needs your attention?	Action step

7. Once you have several different situations, look for themes.
8. Then consider what belief is underneath these emotional experiences. What kind of waffle iron are you using to generate these emotions?
   a. If you need assistance, look back at "Call to Action: What Did I Say to Myself."

Get Emotional About That Life You're Craving

So, what about that life you're craving? That perfect life with fewer bumps and bruises and more good stuff. Suppose it showed up right now. What would you have? More money? More time? More help? Success? Fame? More impact in your career or business? A bigger home? A vacation home? Better health? A smaller waist? Peace of mind? More love? Freedom? Joy?

Wait. I think we might be making progress. The things we crave lead us to our deepest desires.

I'm reminded of a talk with a friend who was concerned that he was behind on building his retirement account. He was worried about how to catch up. Like many of us, he has a vision for where he wants to go in his life, how he wants things to be for himself and his family. We all have dreams of "a better life." We set goals to keep ourselves on track toward our dreams. We create Vision Boards and affirmations. We scour the Internet for the latest tips from self-help gurus on how to manifest our dreams. I turned a closet door into a Vision Board so that I could see it first thing each day and last thing each night. I wanted to give it all the attention that I could so that I could attract the goodies into my life.

Vision Boards are great tools. They get us focused on what's important. They keep us moving toward a goal, offer us inspiration when it seems our vision has gotten cloudy. My first Vision Board was actually a treasure chest. It was a miniature cedar chest. I would cut out pictures of things I wanted, place them in the box and consider them delivered. That's how I got started locating my first emerald birthstone ring.

However, there have been times when it seemed my Vision Board was not working for me. I was focusing on what I wanted but it still seemed elusive. Then, I learned the "behave as if," technique. It's gotten rave reviews. It seems to help get people to access how they would move through the world once they have achieved their goal. I've also tried the "treat what you have as though it is what you want" technique. It's great too. It builds a sense of gratitude and does move you into the idea that what you want is already yours. This certainly makes it easier to locate and manifest. Pretty cool.

But I was fortunate to learn another technique. It's a secret that pumped up my visionary power. I'm talking EXPONENTIAL PUMP UP. In the spirit of reciprocity, sharing the good stuff, I'm bringing this secret to you TODAY. You may have gotten a hint in the opening paragraph. We often set goals to get more things like money, houses, cars, business, etc. But why are these things important to us?

Think about it for a moment. When my friend and I talked about our financial goals and retirement accounts, I asked why the money was important to him. I asked how he would feel if he'd met his retirement account goals. Think about it. Why would you want more money? Or time? My friend really wants freedom and peace of mind. It's not having money sitting around growing bigger in the bank that he craves. It's comfort and peace.

Here's the secret. It's a twist on the "behave as if" strategy. Allow yourself to feel and experience the emotions and state of being that accomplishing your goals, achieving your vision will bring you. How do you want to experience your life each day? Do you want freedom? Peace of mind? Joy? Comfort? Then, "feel as if" you already have these things. This is what you have to claim for yourself. When you look at your Vision Board or repeat your affirmations, allow yourself to feel exactly the way you want to feel when your dreams manifest. What state of being do you want to own? Put yourself in it and wear it like a finely tailored suit or a warm blanket or a superhero outfit. It's yours. Own it.

I've heard many spiritual teachers share a fundamental truth--happiness and joy are our birthright. Life is not intended to be endless struggle. Rather, we are to express and experience the infinite goodness in our universe. The Yoruba of Nigeria in West Africa have a sacred text known as the Odu. It is full of wisdom. One of my favorite Odu verses comments on this very birthright. It's a conversation between the prophet, Orunmila and human beings who're requesting to rest in heaven because going back and forth between heaven and earth is tiring. Yeah, I know you know that feeling. That "Let's just rest in heaven 'cause this life thing is too hard" feeling. Listen to these words from the prophet:

Let us do things with joy.
Those who want to go, let them go.
Orunmila said to the people:
"You cannot avoid going back and
forth to earth,
Until you bring about the good condition that
Olodumare (God) has ordained
for every human being.
After then, you may rest in heaven."
They asked, "What is the good condition?"
Orunmila said: "The good condition
is a good world:
A world in which there is full knowledge
of all things;
Happiness everywhere;
Life without anxiety or fear of enemies;
Without clashes with snakes or other
dangerous animals;
Without fear of death, disease,
litigation, losses;
Without fear of injury from water or fire; and
Without fear of poverty or misery."

Feel that. "The good condition." Wear it. Bathe in it. Peace. Safety. Comfort. Joy. Freedom. Flexibility. Love. This is your birthright. It's divine order. Claim it. Own it. Every moment of every day.

Call to Action ~ Feel the Vision

1. Choose a goal. Think of things that you'll do to get there and the many ways accomplishing this goal will enhance your life.
    a. For example, you may want to start a wellness program. You may get up earlier. Take walks and enjoy the sunrise. You might read something inspirational after your walk. You may eat better food. You might have better muscle tone and flexibility. You may feel more peaceful and have better focus.
2. Be very descriptive about how you will feel once you've accomplished this goal. Then, get into it. Make the feeling a meditation. Notice how your body feels when you have this feeling. Do you smile more? Are you more relaxed? Allow yourself to feel the emotional state that you will have once you reach your goal.
3. You can make a Vision Board for your goal. Be sure to add some feeling statements to it. Use the sight of the words to stimulate peace, comfort, freedom, love or whatever emotional state you want your goal to bring you.

Emotional Rhythm

Burned Out ~ Fried, Died, and Laid to The Side

The thrill is gone. The thrill is gone baby.
The thrill is gone away from me.
~ BB King

When you hear BB King sing these words, you feel them. And Lucille, his guitar, takes that feeling deep inside you. Every inch of your body and soul knows these words.

We've all had days when we could adopt this as our work or business theme song. We greet the day like somebody having a tantrum. We want to stomp our feet and say, "No, no, no. I can't go."

Sometimes, we don't even have to energy to stomp our feet. We're drained, emotionally exhausted. We have nothing to give.

But we will push on. We go through the motions and our heart isn't in our work. In extreme cases, we become distant and impersonal with our clients, team members, and even our family.

This is known as burnout. Yes. Toast, as some would say. If we were hair in my childhood neighborhood, being fried, dyed and laid to the side would be a good thing. This meant you had a fresh hairdo and you were strutting your stuff. You were probably getting ready for a big event where you were going to get lots of compliments. You felt good inside. Getting there may have required some effort but once you look in the mirror...Oh yeah!

But when we reach the point of being fried, we definitely don't feel like strutting our stuff. We don't want any parts of a mirror and if someone paid us a compliment, we'd probably have a hard time believing them. In *Banishing Burnout*, Michael Leitner and Christina Maslach describe it as "lost energy" and "lost enthusiasm."

Christina Maslach created one of the most well-known scales to assess burnout. She even created a version for teachers who are giving of themselves day in and day out. Among those in service oriented fields, burnout is sometimes called compassion fatigue. Maslach's scale measures three things: our level of emotional exhaustion; our feelings of depersonalization AKA going through the motions; and our sense of personal accomplishment at work.

In other words, "Nope. I don't care. This is not working out." Yes, you can hear BB King singing, "The thrill is gone away from me." The love and joy you had for your work or business feels lost.

In order to prevent or manage burnout, we want low emotional exhaustion, low depersonalization, and a high sense of personal accomplishment in our work. This requires a plan.

Emotional engagement is one of the keys to high performance and productivity. A drained, overwhelmed person isn't going to get much done. Once we're in this emotional state, things have gone pretty far down a slippery slope.

You can probably hear your Mama or some other elder saying something like, "A stitch in time saves nine. The early bird catches the worm. An ounce of prevention is worth a pound of cure." Or maybe even, "You slow. You blow."

So, our primary goal is to become aware of the warning signs for burnout and take steps to prevent a spiral into emotional disengagement. In ordering our steps, as my elders would say, we can energize our emotional wellness.

Become familiar with the signs of burnout. Watch for the signs in yourself. Your emotions are signaling you. Common warning signs of burnout of include:

- You feel a loss of excitement about your work.
- You feel emotionally drained by your work responsibilities.
- You're irritable with clients, partners, co-workers.
- You feel disconnected. Work feels like you're just going through the motions.
- You're not clear what's going right in your business or work.
- You're more focused on setbacks than on accomplishments.
- You don't feel fulfilled. Your work doesn't hold meaning for you.

I spent a significant part of my career working with HIV/AIDS care providers. As you might imagine, burnout was a significant risk before treatment advances helped patients live longer and healthier lives. I provided stress management training to healthcare providers all over the world. One of the things that I encouraged them to do was to make a list of their signs and symptoms that things were heading downhill. I also encouraged them to partner with other providers to help each other build awareness. The strategy was to make a list of your signs and symptoms and share it with a trusted co-worker. When the other person noticed you were doing something on your list, they could call your attention to it or simply wave the list like a white flag of surrender. Hopefully, this would help bring some levity to the situation and healing could begin.

One of the things that I learned from doing this work is that preventing and managing burnout requires a multi-level approach. Interventions are necessary from the individual through the family to the community environment and beyond. The individual needs to hone their awareness and select strategies that help them re-center and recover. They need the support of family members at home and a partnership with co-workers and supervisors to create work environments that nurture wellness. Some countries, like Botswana, take workplace wellness so seriously that they're willing to build a national program.

You can start by tuning into your awareness and selecting strategies to help you use your emotional signals. Ask yourself, what are my emotions telling me? Be sure to listen for the answers. Close your eyes, if needed. Go to a park. Find a quiet space and listen to you.

In "The Thrill is Gone," BB King sings, "Someday I know I'll be moving on...I'm free from your spell." Or, as my elders would say, "Trouble don't last always." With a few well-placed strategies, you can prevent and manage burnout. Make a plan. Build the emotional energy you need to grow the work that matters most to you.

Call to Action ~ Time Out

Taking time out is one of the best ways to recover. Learn when it's time to step away.

1. Make two lists.
    a. On one write your stress/burnout signals.
    b. On the second list, include strategies that help you find calm, breathe, make clear decisions, rescue you from emotional drain, and remain emotionally energized.
2. Then, do a mix and match.
    a. Choose a strategy to help you manage each signal that you need a break, a breather, a time-out.
    b. Identify at 2-3 strategies that work for each symptom. Then, tryout some new ones.
3. Make re-grouping a part of your daily routine.

How Do You Want to Feel Day In and Day Out?

How we spend our days is, of course, how we spend our lives. ~ *Annie Dillard*

Repeat that quote a couple of times. "How we spend our days is, of course, how we spend our lives." "How we spend our days is, of course, how we spend our lives."

It's a wake-up call. It reminds us that what we're doing today has the power to define our lives. The question is, what do you want to do today?

How do you want this day to end? How do you want to feel? Accomplished? Vibrant? Peaceful? Satisfied? Confident? Pleased? Energized? Ready? Decisive?

What resources do you need to get there? Of course, you need time, money, and people to help you. Yeah, you might want the traffic to be lighter or a deadline to be extended.

But how will you manage your emotional energy so that you end this day feeling the way you want to feel? Your emotions are one of your most powerful resources. Think about it. How many times have you said to yourself, "I don't have the energy for that." Or perhaps you said, "I'm not feeling it."

These words make it clear that you've taken stock and you know, "That's not gonna happen." How do we conserve, reserve, and build our emotional energy to get us where we want to be? To feel the way we want to feel every day?

In their book, *Powered by Feel: How Individuals, Teams, and Companies Excel*, James G. S. Clawson and Doug Newburg describe how the way you feel drives your level of excellence. They share research from countless interviews with world-class athletes, artists, organizations, leaders, healthcare providers, and people considered to be peak performers in their work or area of expertise. A common strategy in this group was that they chose goals based on how they wanted to feel every day rather than as a means to an end. Their goals weren't based upon amassing money or notoriety. Rather, they stayed connected to how they wanted to feel. For many of them, the feeling of total engagement in their work was their marker for success.

Clawson and Newburg coined the phenomenon, "Professionals will do what they have to do regardless of how they feel," (PWD WTHTD ROHTD). They say this is a "formula for mediocrity," because it robs people of choice. It chains them to obligation and results in reduced energy. In this modus operandi, we go about getting it all done, no matter how we feel. As our energy gauge is headed toward drained, we offer empty smiles and fake compliance. We ignore our internal signals. We're disconnected.

"PWD WTHD ROHTD" deprives us of one of our most powerful energy sources, our emotions. We could change the P in this acronym to M for Mamas/Mommies/Mothers or W for women or S for Sistahs. I've watched moms skip their health-care appointments but diligently take their children for regular care. Women are often taught to put everyone's needs before their own, to sacrifice their self-care and remain silent about their discomfort. Sistahs (black women), plagued by the "strong black woman" stereotype, are often taught to bear pain in silence. And no, never ask for assistance. Just get the job done. When we're numb, moving like a robot on skates, and simply doing things to get them done, we cannot access our passion, the fuel for peak performance, meaning and fulfillment in our everyday life.

We can be proactive about our emotional energy, staying connected to what enhances our interactions and productivity. This means that we need a love relationship with what we do, whether it's related to work, family, or some other area or our lives. Your passion is not as much about what you're doing as it is about how doing that thing gets deep inside you. Where does it touch you? How does it arouse your deepest love for it? Why does it get inside your heart? Think about how what you're doing touches your heart.

I once heard a friend say that George Washington Carver was a great scientist because he was "in love" with what he was doing. I doubt anyone before or since him knows more about peanuts and what they can do. I'm imagining this great give and take conversation between Carver and peanuts. He tries something. That's like his pick-up line. He waits. What will the peanut say? Is it interested?

The peanut's reaction is really a verbal response, an invitation to go deeper or try something different. Eventually, the peanut shows Carver, it can transform from food to fuel to cosmetic and more. It gives Carver a whole lot of love. And Carver loves it right back.

Our emotions allow us to connect with what we're doing and use our inner resources to bring our best to it. What steps will you take to love what you do in your life and get your life to love you right back? Choose how you want to feel and make love to that feeling.

Call to Action ~ How Do You Want to Feel?

1. Decide on the end of your day--When you awaken, decide how you want to feel at the end of your day. Pick a word for the day.

   Peaceful. Vibrant. Satisfied. Energized. Accomplished. Fulfilled. Aligned. Organized. Nurtured. Supported. Rested. Relieved.

   The list is endless. Looking at what's on your schedule for the day can help you make the best choice. After all is said and done, how do you want to feel? Make sure you choose something that energizes you, helps you focus, and make the choices that you need to move smoothly through your day.

   Put your word on a post-it note. Set reminders on your phone. Put notes on your computer screen.

   As the day progresses, check in with yourself and notice how you're feeling. Is what you're doing helping you to get that feeling you want to have at the end of the day? If not, re-arrange.

   Managing our emotional energy is our personal balancing act. While we might be able to teach a juggler or tightrope walker a few things, we're not interested in our lives becoming a circus.

In order to give our best, we may need to move things around. Or shift our focus. Or switch tasks. Know how you want to feel. Notice if you're on that path. Then, re-route as needed.

Call to Action ~ Emotional Ups and Downs

1. Make an "Up and Down" list – Draw a line down the middle of a sheet of paper. Write Up at the top of one column and Down at the top of the other column. After you complete an activity, take note of how you feel. If you feel energized, ready to move on, inspired, joyful, focused or up, write the activity in the Up column. If you feel drained, bothered, overwhelmed, or bogged down, write the activity in the Down column.

   If it's easier, use your smart phone. Create a note for your Up and one for Down activities. Use the easiest strategy to keep track of your activities. You're a detective on a mission to locate your emotional energy drains and your emotional energy boosters.

   After several days, preferably one week, review your lists. Consider these questions:

   a. What can you rearrange?

   b. For those things that are draining consider:

    i. How can you get help with or eliminate the energy drains?
    ii. What can you delegate?
    iii. What can you do differently?
c. How can you do more of the things that leave you feeling energized?

Emotional Flexibility

Stuck on Repeat in a Comfort Zone

There are many of us who believe that vinyl albums can make a comeback. You know, the ones that you play on a turntable. I know I'm dating myself but I still have some of my favorite music on vinyl.

I logged a lot of hours at the bargain table in many a record store. I got some great deals. No, I did not throw them out yet. And yes, my turntable can make a comeback.

But you have to be careful with vinyl because if you scratch it, the record gets stuck in the same spot. And the phrase or beat repeats over and over something like this, "My baby...My baby...My baby...My baby..." This goes on until someone intervenes and moves the needle.

It's the same way when we get into our worrying or overthinking groove. We replay the same thought and feeling. Or when we do things the same way because it's the way we've always done it. It's our standard practice. But just like the record, we can't move forward.

In this groove, we're often focused on what we fear or what could go wrong or what is wrong or how difficult it is to change. One of the places that I get stuck is in my criticism of things I want to improve. Sometimes I'm so stuck on what's not right that I miss what's going well.

For example, I want to let go of a few pounds. I'm looking in the mirror saying things like, "These pants don't fit right," or "Oh, this back fat has to go!" But then someone will compliment me and say, "What a nice outfit!" Or, "I really like those colors," Or, "You always look so nice."

Like many women, I still sometimes have to resist the tendency to pull out the double-barrel shotgun and blow that compliment right out of the air. You know how we do it. We get a compliment and we start trying to convince the person why it's not accurate. Or we point out something that's not right.

When I'm only focusing on what's not right, I'm missing what's going well. When I'm stuck on what's wrong, I'm out of balance and off balance. And I'm no longer focused on getting to my goal of releasing weight. I'm only focusing on how I'm retaining weight.

I can't use all of my resources because I'm not paying attention to what I have available to me. I'm not recognizing that no matter what size I am, I do things that are good for my body and my appearance. I'm stuck. I fear that I can't get where I really want to go.

Sometimes we'd rather stay stuck because we fear that once we get what we want, we'll lose. We've been back and forth between our goal and the same spot so many times that we'd rather just hold on to what we think is inevitable. Or in my case, I'd lost and gained the same 10 pounds so many times, I thought there was no way to get out of the pattern. Same place, different day.

Other times we're not moving because we're in what's known as a comfort zone. I think of them as places that offer protection. Places where we can play it safe. Some say that comfort zones help us avoid the risks that are necessary for growth. Comfort zones keep us from "putting ourselves out there." As such, we're most likely "pinned in," or "backed into a corner." Instead of growing, we get stuck.

We may still be active but there's stagnation. No movement outward or upward. No growth. Energy does not expand or flow in this place. Here's the thing. Taking a risk is the only way out. I'm reminded of one of my favorite quotes:

"The time came when the risk it took to remain tight inside a bud was more painful than the risk it took to blossom."
~ (most often credited to Anais Nin, also credited to Elizabeth Appell)

Growing is a natural and unavoidable experience. However, if we decide to defy Mother Nature, the pain of avoiding growth will worsen over time. In fact, it will probably become so awful and so intense that we will dislike being "pinned in," and safe, much more than we dislike stepping out of our comfort zone or ending that deafening repeat.

Eventually, unless we go completely numb, the unpleasantness of stagnation will be much greater and louder than the unpleasantness that we associate with taking a risk. In the end, making a move is the lesser of the evils. We will opt to take a chance on our growth. We will move the needle and take the risk on our dreams.

Indeed, the pain will become a source of motivation. We will be energized to move out of our comfort zone, which brings us to this insightful guidance from Dr. Michael B. Beckwith:

"Pain pushes us until vision pulls us."

Pain can get behind us, inside us, around us and give us a push forward. Our desire to escape or lessen the discomfort will get us going. However, something quite magical and wonderful happens once we start moving away from pain. We begin to get clarity on where we want to go.

Pain actually helps us define our joy and expand our idea of comfort. It shows us exactly what we don't want so that we can define what we do want. This is what Thich Nhat Haln calls transforming our suffering into our joy and happiness. Our vision of our best self grows creating momentum and flow in our movement. We're going toward what we want. We're building what matters to us. Here is where risk-taking and comfort work together. We actually grow in our comfort with taking risks.

When we merge our comfort zone with risk-taking, confidence and faith, it expands. When our challenges and our strengths are working together, we have energy flow. Change can take place.

So, I've learned to use the urge to shoot down a compliment as a reminder to shift my focus. When I feel this urge, I pause. The urge now becomes my fuel for moving in a more productive direction. In the beginning, I would literally say to myself, "Change your focus." That morphed into "Accept the compliment." The compliment is my reminder of what's going right. I relax. I notice my confidence and my competence.

When we get stuck, here's one of the most powerful moves we can make. Use our feelings as a reminder to change our focus. Our eyes open to our strengths, skills, and other assets. We find balance and energy to go toward our goal.

The next time your record gets stuck, make shift happen.

Call to Action ~ Make Shift Happen

1. Consider these questions:
    a. How would you like to expand your comfort zone to increase your growth and productivity?
    b. Where do you get stuck on emotional repeat?
2. Expand your comfort zone.
    a. Write three things you can do to get more comfortable with taking risks.
    b. Here's one to get you started. When you're launching a new project:
        i. Get feedback from family, friends, and colleagues before you launch a new project.
        ii. Use their feedback to make improvements and boost your confidence energy.
    c. What are at least two other things you can do to expand your comfort zone?

3. Move the needle on your repeating emotion.
    a. Identify the emotion, a situation where it's likely to show up, and what you say to yourself when you're stuck.
    b. Notice how you're using the emotional repeat to protect yourself from a fear of failure or some other thing that you worry could happen.
        i. You've been here before. Consider what you've learned and how you can use it to shift.
    c. Identify a small shift in focus that you can implement when you're stuck. Create a shift that will help you maintain your optimism about moving toward your goal.

Feelings Are Smart

You've probably heard people say, "A little fear is a good thing." Or something like "A little fear will keep you alert, aware, and thinking about your next best move." These statements refer to the idea that our emotions can help us problem solve and use our inner resources wisely.

Some might say moderation is the key. We all know what happens when our fear, self-doubt, or other challenging emotions get too intense. We become paralyzed, unable to move forward. Thoughts of things that frighten and worry us flood our minds.

We tend to jump ahead and create an even more frightening story. Our thoughts and emotions snowball into a horror story with us and our family destitute or some other awful scenario. As this story is spinning in our heads, our hearts are racing, our breathing is speeding and we're sweating or tingling.

We're on a rollercoaster. We're paralyzed and more likely to choose solutions that don't fit the problem. Or we might choose to avoid the problem.

We need to get off the rollercoaster and find the teeter-totter or see-saw quickly. Balance is one of the keys to making the best use of our emotional energy. Modulating and regulating our emotions creates flexibility and allows us to shift our attention and focus on what matters most in any given moment. We're in a position to use our emotional resources wisely.

Good self-awareness is essential. We have to recognize when we've tipped the emotion scales too far. We need to know how to dial our emotions up or down as needed. You may have heard the term emotional intelligence or EQ. Psychologists John Mayer and Peter Salovey first used the term. Daniel Goleman has become well-known for his writing on the topic and synthesizing the research for our daily use. He prefers EI as the abbreviation for this concept.

Bradberry and Greaves report that emotional intelligence got widespread attention when researchers realized that high IQ (measured intelligence/cognitive skills) did not assure greater success. Yes, people with very high IQ scores often outperformed people with average scores. But people with average scores outperformed people with high scores more often. As with all research, this led to more questions. What did the average people have that gave them the edge more often than the high scorers? Emotional intelligence emerged from research aimed at answering this question.

In essence, emotional intelligence is a set of skills or competencies as described by Goleman. He offers a four-part model: self-awareness, self-management, social awareness, and relationship management. These four domains fit broadly in the categories of self and relationships. Each domain includes a set of competencies such as emotional self-awareness, emotional balance, positive outlook, adaptability, empathy, mentorship, conflict management, inspiration, and teamwork, among others.

What does emotional intelligence look like? It includes the ability to:

- recognize our own and others' emotions
- identify emotional triggers
- monitor and regulate our emotions
- know our strengths and challenges
- understand how we impact others
- respond with empathy
- build rapport with others

Looking at this list makes it easy to see how EQ can enhance our quality of life at home, work, and play. Reduced stress, better work performance, improved relationships, and enhanced wellness are among the benefits noted by some researchers. Others say EQ is too difficult to measure for a true scientific evaluation.

Be we don't really need much science to recognize that our emotions are valuable resources. EQ helps us regulate our emotional energy and make the most of it.

Call to Action ~ Raise Your Awareness

Get to know your emotional patterns. Build your self-awareness.

1. Identify one of your emotional triggers.
    a. This is something that begins to tip your emotional scale. It could be a tone of voice, a look, a work responsibility, an expectation or any number of things.
    b. What feeling emerges in you? Fear. Anger. Disgust. Indifference.
    c. Whatever the feeling, recognize it and notice what it's telling you.
2. Your thoughts support your emotional response to this trigger. So, identify what you're saying to yourself and why this particular thing rubs you the wrong way.
    a. It could be a person who reminds you of a childhood experience or another setting where you faced a similar person.
    b. It could be a task that stimulates concerns about embarrassment or failure?
3. Once you know your triggers and why, you can begin to gently move yourself toward emotional balance.

a. If you're caught up in a past experience, bring yourself to the now. This is a different situation. What small change can you make to get a shift in your emotional experience?

Emotional Connection

One of The Easiest Things You Can Do and Feel

Count your blessings. Say thank you. I know your grandmama or great auntie or Mama or Big Mama or Ms. Fannie or some elder has told you some version of "count your blessings." My Mama Louise had a funny way of reminding us to be thankful and to thank others. She'd say, "you can tell a dog thank you," or "they didn't even say thank you dog." You get it. Thank you is one of the easiest things you can say.

Like many of us, as a child you may have ended your day with nightly prayers or affirmations. The adults in your life coached you to say what you were thankful for and to ask for special blessings for those you love. If you ever forgot to say thank you, your caregivers reminded you until it became a seamless practice.

When we look back on these early practices, we think about them as our elders' efforts to help us build good character or be kind and generous people. But today researchers have joined the ranks of those touting the power of gratitude. And if you're a parent, you'll love this. Some research indicates that teens who practiced gratitude were described as more hopeful. They had greater life satisfaction and were less likely to be involved in cheating, drinking, or drug use.

Gratitude has been reliably associated with a range of emotional, physical, and relationship benefits. Emotional benefits include increased happiness, more peace of mind, reduced stress, and better stress management. Being grateful leaves us feeling better, happier, and more peaceful. When we go through tough times, we may be better able to recover.

Being grateful is associated with health benefits and a desire to exercise. Gratitude seems to be the gift that keeps on giving, since exercise is associated with improved heart health among other physiological advantages. Physical benefits related to a gratitude practice include improved immune function, enhanced cardio-vascular health including lower blood pressure, and better sleep cycles.

Gratitude helps us see the good in others and the ways they make our lives better. Seeing the wonderful ways others impact our lives seems to make us more caring and more likely to practice forgiveness in our relationships. Interpersonal benefits include greater compassion for others and increased ability to forgive others.

But here's another way that I've used my gratitude practice. There have been times when I was so physically tired that I went below zero. It seemed that some little gremlins kept adding things with deadlines to my TO DO list. Extra family and work responsibilities were multiplying. They were like dung beetles that roll up into little balls. Before you know it that one beetle becomes many beetles crawling everywhere.

When I have to maneuver my way back above zero, I meditate. I practice Qigong. A lot. A whole lot. I eat foods that nourish the five major energy systems in my body. I pray. I remind myself of my truth, my "why," several times a day. I repeat affirmations. I have faith. I set goals. I make plans for getting things done. I put things in order. I give myself permission to do a little at a time. I remember what's important to me. I rest. I take walks. I say no to things that can wait or never happen. I spend time with old friends who've loved me for a long time. I am kind and gentle with myself.

On one trip back from zero, I decided that it was time to step up my gratitude practice. I felt like I had nothing left, so I took a deep dive into the riches in my life. Being thankful is one of the easiest things you can do. When you're at the bottom of the barrel, you need easy things to do. I set my mind on finding the good, all the things that I had to be thankful for, all the little treasures that were hiding behind my never-ending list of deadlines.

In addition to meditating on what I was thankful for or writing it down, I started sharing my list publicly. I redesigned my #GratitudeEveryday program. Every day I created a quote about something I was thankful for and I posted them on social media. Then, I asked people to share what they were thankful for with me.

I felt good when I shared my list. But when somebody liked a post or responded with something from their gratitude list, I smiled. My heart did a happy dance and I felt even more of what made that particular thing so wonderful.

And ooooohhhh! How powerful was the impact on my well-being? We couldn't measure it.

Gratitude worked. I got an energy boost. I became so much more aware of how all the things that I'm grateful for make me feel alive, present, joyful, capable, recharged, secure, supported, loved, confident, safe, prosperous, free, and magical.

Yeah, you get the feeling.

I know that I've said it before. I've told you that gratitude will improve you mental and physical health. And I know your grandmama told you to count your blessings but here's what I invite you to do today.

Get into the feeling of #GratitudeEveryday. How does being thankful leave you feeling? How does that thing you're thankful for light the fire in your heart?

Check out this quote and get fired up about your life every day.

> *"Gratitude unlocks the fullness of life. It turns what we have into enough, and more. It turns denial into acceptance, chaos to order, confusion to clarity. It can turn a meal into a feast, a house into a home, a stranger into a friend. Gratitude makes sense of our past, brings peace for today, and creates a vision for tomorrow."*
> *- Melody Beattie*

Call to Action ~ Be Thankful

Use your gratitude to spark your joy. Here are a few activities that you can practice to stoke your fire.

1. If you like to journal, keep a gratitude journal. It can be a paper or digital journal. Do

it every day. It's a great morning and evening practice.

2. Consider making a gratitude jar. Write your "thankful for" notes on different colored paper and place them in a large jar. Periodically, fish around in the jar and read a few of them.
3. If you like to meditate, practice gratitude meditation. Close your eyes a few times a day. Take a few deep breaths. Relax and simply visualize all the things you're thankful for. Really let yourself feel gratitude. Allow yourself to get into the feelings, the sights and sounds, and all the sensory experiences associated with that moment. As the feeling grows, so will your awareness of peace.
4. Say thank you to others. When you say thank you, engage with the other person or people. Look at them in their eyes, shake their hand, smile. Let them know you really appreciate them. Put your heart into it.
5. Create a gratitude collage. This can be a small, framed collage or a large poster board. Choose what works for you. Be creative with colors that appeal to you. Place it on your wall to remind you of events, people, places, or things that you truly appreciate. Or take a

photograph and make it the wallpaper on your smart phone or computer.

6. Write down your accomplishments. Keep track of the ways that you grow and improve. Be thankful for you.
7. Even at times when it seems life is crazy and not making much sense, look for the gift. What can you be thankful for in your experience?
    a. Maybe a traffic jam slowed you down just long enough to drive up to your meeting and get a perfect parking spot.

Emotional Energy Chart

Emotional Energy Recharge, Renew, Replenish	
Emotional Wisdom	Tune in to emotions as signals and guidance.
Emotional Rhythm	Decide how you want to feel and create it.
Emotional Flexibility	Explore shifts that expand your comfort zone.
Emotional Connection	Practice gratitude. Stay connected to the good in your life.

RECOVER YOUR BODY MIND SPIRIT

Spiritual Energy

Our spirit is as real and as tangible as our body. Spirit sits at the core of our being guiding us along the way and connecting us to life around us. Everyone from spiritual teachers to physicists say that we're a part of something bigger. Not only are we connected but we play a significant part in the life web that sustains us each day. Your spirit came to life in your body for a reason. At your deepest level, you are here to do some magical good that only you can do. In this section, we apply our four strategies--Wisdom, Rhythm, Flexibility and Connection--to the process of building, sustaining and renewing spritual energy.

Get intimate with your life purpose. Find the super-person living inside you and give them a name. Think deeply about the problems that you want to solve. Learn how to stay connected to the spiritual wisdom you've had all of your life.

Discover the many ways that your purpose can impact the world. Learn how purpose makes your day, enhances your health, and helps you define your missions. Let purpose become the beat that brings rhythm to the many roles you play in life.

Trust the power of your purpose. Some of our most powerful resources are invisible. Have faith in the impact that you can have in the world. Let your faith lead you to patience and flexibility as you move along your life path.

Open yourself up to the power that everyone's life purpose is intimately connected. Build teams that help members thrive in fulfilling their purpose. Acknowledge your purpose is a power tool for crafting a legacy of good in the world. Find meaning and let your life outlive you.

Spiritual Wisdom

You Did That on Purpose

When I was a child growing up in one of Atlanta's oldest communities, we often used the phrase, "You did that on purpose." The statement indicated intentionality in someone's actions. Their behavior was not accidental but executed with forethought, sometimes malicious forethought. However, there was another, often unspoken, meaning to doing something on purpose. This was a subtler communication from my parents and elders that our lives have meaning. We are destined to do and be in the world in such a way that uplifts, heals, and elevates other people and our community.

In psychological, philosophical and religious literature, these ideas fall within the realm of existentialism or eudaimonic well-being. I know. That's lots of big words. Don't rush off to Google or dictionary.com right now. Basically, it boils down to human striving to find meaning in our lives, specifically meaning rooted in our spirituality, our sense of connection to life, people, nature, and the universe.

In our everyday lives, especially in the world of those committed to wellness, we may hear people use the phrase, “I’m living my life on purpose.” It’s their mantra or proclamation of a commitment to stay focused on behaviors and mindsets that cultivate their best self--in mind and body. Building an overall sense of wellness from one day to the next is most often the aim. That includes staving off those extra pounds that always seem to be chasing us down, taking a breath before speaking when a co-worker does yet another immeasurably irritating thing, and regularly reminding ourselves that our health matters. A strong, fit mind and body are certainly essential to living “on purpose.” Health in our minds and bodies gives our spirit a peaceful and thriving house to live in but the spirit has its own unique work to do.

If you grew up Christian, you probably heard the phrase your body is a temple for the spirit. My Taoist teacher says that each spirit chooses the body it needs to fulfill its unique purpose on earth. The Yoruba sacred text says those chosen to bring good into the world are called human beings, each of whom chooses a destiny to complete on earth. Further, that destiny is designed to help human beings achieve the good condition.

While some suggest that striving for meaning is more important than striving for happiness, the Yoruba sacred texts indicate that our spirits choose our journeys with joy. I love it! Yes, you can have both. You can be "on purpose," and joy-full. This is not to suggest there won't be challenges on your journey. However, when you're "on purpose," any experience can be an opportunity to locate the good that will propel you forward.

People often ask me, "How can someone find their life purpose?" Or, "How do you know what your purpose is?" Within a split second, I'm usually flooded with a colorful assortment of ideas for self-exploration. Simultaneously, I'm swaddled in a deep feeling of joy because of my belief that everyone has some good that only they brought to the world. I'm basking in delight that they want to be conscious, fully aware of what they came to the world to do.

Sometimes I hear Teddy Pendergrass singing, "You can't hide from yourself. Everywhere you go there you are." Other times, I imagine Fannie Lou Hamer singing This Little Light of Mine. Teddy Pendergrass sang that the "truth is the light, a light shining within." Throughout my life, I've sung alone and with others, "This little light of mine, I'm gonna let it shine...everywhere I go, I'm gonna let it shine."

Both songs remind us of a fundamental truth. We are light, energy, the power to create. Quantum physicists agree that at the deepest level every living thing is energy. This energy is intelligent and indestructible. It has the capacity to take infinite forms. We chose our physical form so that we could bring some special good into the world. So, let your light shine from the inside out. The world is a better place because you are here.

"Let light come from the inside out; otherwise, you're always looking for the spotlight." ~Dr. Nan Lu.

Call to Action ~ Living on Purpose

I'm very aware that there are probably at least as many ways to know your purpose, as there are people. We won't be able to explore all nine billion of them here. But here are a few fun ways to identify and connect to your purpose. Enjoy!

1. Sentence Completion
    a. Complete this sentence: I was born to ____________________.
    b. Helpful hints:
        i. Think about what you would do even if you weren't paid for it. No, this is not hanging at the beach or never working another day in your life.

ii. This is what you feel passionate about, the work, the activities that ignite your fire.

iii. Remember - A job is not a purpose. You may work as an accountant, but filing tax returns is not your purpose. However, teaching people about wealth building and helping them recognize abundance as their birthright would be moving in the direction of a life purpose. Perhaps, you're an abundance educator.

2. What's in a Name?

"A name is an important word with meaning and energy that identifies someone or something. Our names bring certain patterns to our lives and have the capacity to forge our destinies...It's a code ingrained in us that allows us, when it is called to remember, recognize, and respond to our purpose."—Sobonfu Some

a. Names and nicknames often give us clues about who we came to the world to be. In many cultures, we're given a name that reminds us of our spirit's choice of purpose. For example, my grandmother named my father David and my uncle Alexander because she wanted them to be great. She believed they were destined for greatness. Perhaps your friends and family call you Preacher because of your ability to inspire others or Boss because you're a natural leader, able to organize a range of talents and skills so people blend together like finely tuned instruments.

b. What does your name reveal? Ask caregivers and relatives how you got your name. Google your name. Research. Become a detective on a search for meaning in your name. Think about how it connects to your deepest passions.

3. Fired Up
   a. Answer these questions:
      i. What were the things that got you excited as a kid? What pretend games did you play?
      ii. What work or activities get you most excited about being alive? Are you a banker who enjoys her 9-5 but really loves coaching kids at soccer or baseball or basketball? Perhaps, you feel most alive when you are teaching others a skill or leading a dance class or gardening. Maybe you're motivated by watching someone smile or bob their

head when you sing or read poetry. Or you may like to build houses or decorate them and put in those little conveniences that make people feel comfortable and warm and loved.

b. What work would you absolutely love to do if you had unlimited resources and you could do anything in the world?
    i. Example: I would travel the world building schools and making sure all children had access to the best quality education.
    ii. I would design wellness programs and teach people how to incorporate wellness into their lives even as their lives and circumstances change.
c. How would you summarize that work or its impact in 1 – 2 words?
    i. Examples: Teacher, Thought Leader, Change Agent, Wellness Educator, Genius Catalyst, Liberation Specialist, Freedom Fighter, Healer, Life Designer, Style Simulator, Beauty Cultivator, Earth Worker, Peacemaker, Scientist, Spiritual Scientist, Abundance Educator, Builder, Inspirational Speaker.

4. What if?
    a. What if you had a magical ability to transport yourself beyond our time-space continuum where you could see everything that has occurred and all the choices available to you? Imagine that you are in the fifth dimension looking at your whole life. As you look over your life, notice there's a group of people gathering for a banquet. They're all dressed up in their finest. Someone is about to be honored with a lifetime achievement award. That someone is you. What's the reason for the award? What great thing have you done?
    b. Think about it. What if you were receiving a lifetime achievement award? Why would others be recognizing you? What do you want to accomplish within your lifetime? What problems do you want to solve? How have you added value to the world? As you take a look over your life from the fifth dimension, how is your light shining?
    c. From the fifth dimension, as you watch yourself walking up to receive your award, what do you say? Complete this acceptance speech: Thank you so much for this honor. I am filled with joy to receive the lifetime

achievement award for _______________ ___________________________. Fill in some details. Discuss why you embarked on the work that led to the achievement. Describe how it made your heart sing. Share how you moved through challenges. What was your guiding light? Why would you do it all over again?

Spiritual Rhythm

How Many Hats Do You Wear?

What's your answer to this question? I'm guessing that you can think of two or three or eight different hats that you wear. My maternal grandmother, "Mother," was a natural at wearing hats, literally and figuratively. She was a master chef, baker, and a public speaker. Not to mention a fabulous, bomb-diggity grandmother and a fashionista. She was "all that and a bag of chips." (I know. I'm dating myself. Today, young people would probably say something about something being on fleek or lit. But I digress.)

Mother was known for her ornate hats. She was a connoisseur of fine millinery. She had personal relationships with top hat designers. I've always said that she could put a bowl of fruit on her head and people would drool over how good she looked. Some looked like a bullfighter would don them while others were certainly crowns worn by royalty in very exotic places. And she was comfortable in every one of them. Today, we would say that her hats were the signatures for her brand. Her hats were made of everything from feathers to felt. Often made of the same fabric as her dress or suit, they were like a logo symbolizing her genius, eloquence, and elegance.

People wanted to be at the table with my grandmother. To eat her food. To hear her ideas and be inspired. You see, it didn't matter whether she was cooking or speaking. She was always feeding people, nurturing us with food or ideas.

She had an understanding of food that mystifies the average grocery shopper. She knew how to bring out the best in every food that she cooked. The baking temperature, the spices added, the timing of everything from beginning to end. Yummy. (Yes, my mouth is watering.) Once she said that Pa Jones (her husband in later life) didn't know how to treat spaghetti. It was as though spaghetti was a person with a certain temperament in need of special care. Pa Jones attempted to reheat leftover spaghetti and it was sticky. The food wasn't at its best and Mother knew exactly what went wrong.

As a public speaker, she touched people's hearts. For part of my childhood, she lived in Chicago. But she was a sought-after Women's Day speaker at churches in our community. She would return to Atlanta and step into church with hat, coat, dress, purse, and shoes all made of the same fabric. And she wasn't in the least bit pretentious. You could just as easily find her scrubbing pots or caring for my great-grandmother. But when she came as the keynote speaker, she dressed the part. And she captured hearts. Her metaphors created a personal connection for her audience. I remember being mesmerized as she gave a speech about a nail and connected it to the bible and faith and rising to the best in you. She was poetic, powerful, and moving.

Mother was an excellent example of being centered in one's purpose while having many missions. It didn't matter whether she was cooking, speaking, or making a fashion statement. Her goal was clear: Bring out the best.

- Bring out the best in food.
- Bring out the best in people.
- Bring out the best in myself.

The singular purpose connects multiple missions. Yeah. Take a breath. Whew! You can really do it all if you have a plan, if you're tuned into the glue that holds it all together.

You've probably been drained wondering how can I be all these things to all these people? Mom, spouse, entrepreneur, yogi, architect, runner, swimmer,

CEO, shopper, cook, designer, you name it. You've got multiple roles.

Once you know your purpose, it becomes the thread that connects everything you do, including the dishes. Clarity of purpose gives you a sense of order, a rhythm. It's the drumbeat that you march to around the clock.

It's the core that anchors you so that you can spread out. The mom in you has something in common with you the entrepreneur. The entrepreneur has something in common with you the volunteer. The volunteer has something in common with the yogi in you. As you think about these different roles, you might begin to see how each one informs the other. The skillsets and emotional connections you use in each one helps you in the other roles.

When you take the time to connect your missions with your purpose, you can map your course and move forward with precision. You wear many hats. You can look good and feel good wearing every one of them. The truth is that your purpose will literally make your day.

Make My Day

I know that title sounds like something out of a Clint Eastwood *Dirty Harry* movie. Like fighting words. But not this time. There's no sarcasm.

The words really capture my intended message. When you have a reason, a purpose, that guides your life, it makes your day. Every day.

Purpose is the "why," that ignites your passion, energizes your mind, body, and spirit. It expands your vision in ways that leave you no choice but to take action and make your life beautiful. When we connect our purpose to our actions, it guides us to decisions that make sense for a meaningful and fulfilling life.

In *Black Hole Focus*, Isaiah Hankel describes a group of people in Okinawa who live active lives past the age of 100. They're teaching karate and learning to fish and doing all sorts of things like every day is their chance to grow. They do this despite the fact that based on age many of us would say their golden years have long gone. They don't have a word for retirement, but they do have very low rates of diseases like breast and colon cancer.

And get this. I listened to Dan Buettner's TED Talk, *How to Live to be 100+*. In it he discusses his research on "Blue Zones," places where people live healthy lives past the age of 100. Buettner said that most Okinawans die peacefully in their sleep. What was the last thing they did before closing their eyes for the last time? Yes, they had sexual intercourse. Definitely. Let your last moments on earth be filled with a loving exchange.

What's their secret? Ikigai. It's the idea that guides their daily life. In essence, the English translation would be "the reason that I wake up in the morning." They live every day with a certainty that it holds fulfillment. Scholars suggest that the central role of purpose in their lives may enhance their overall well-being. Their lower incidence of deadly diseases may be related to their dedication to purpose, their ability to connect life's activities to their sense of meaning. They're showing us that purpose may not only give you a reason and make your day. It may just boost your health.

This sense of ease about purpose stands in stark contrast to conversations that I've had with many people. For example, in conversations with college students, I ask what they want to do, what kind of career interests them. They say things like work with children, work in human resources, help people who have mental illnesses, or conduct research to learn more about how the brain works.

However, very few of them can tell me why they want to do these things. Of course, some will express the belief this work will help them make money. Others will say they like helping people. Still others will say their mom or dad told them it's the best thing to do to make money. But none of them have ever told me that what they want to do is connected to their purpose or desire for meaning and fulfillment.

In fact, I have yet to meet a student who can tell me their purpose. They say, "I haven't found it yet." Or, "I think I'm too young to know." And college students aren't the only people who tell me that they don't know their purpose. I've had the same conversations with adults. Many have felt lost for much of their lives. They've had jobs that they enjoyed but they never felt their work was connected to their purpose. They've spent a significant portion of their lives feeling as though something was missing.

So, I go on a treasure hunt with them searching for why the work they want to do or have done holds enough importance to them to go for it and stick with it. On these treasure hunts, we're looking for their why. I mean their deep-down sense of how this work you want to do or that they did for many years connects to their reason for being, living, and doing every day. Because in the end, that's the reason we will keep going and growing in the work we choose to do.

And the work we do is not limited to our career. We do all kinds of work in our daily lives. In one webinar about finding your soul's purpose, a presenter surprised me. He said that everything we do in our lives supports our purpose. He said that all the tasks we engage in help us to fulfill our soul's purpose, including sweeping the floor.

If you're like me, laundry is not on the top of your list of favorite activities. Maybe loading the dishwasher or vacuuming or downsizing your closet is your least favorite task. It might seem like a big leap to consider these tasks as essential, even necessary, to our being the person we came to the world to be. But the idea held promise for me. I mean, I can use a little something to put some magic into sweeping or doing laundry. So, this presenter had my attention.

He encouraged listeners to think about how sweeping our floor, caring for our home or other seemingly mundane, pro forma tasks are related to our life purpose. Listen, that mythology class that you took in college might seem really useless until you're in an interview with a potential employer or client who has artwork related to your course. Or you listen to a myth and it offers a solution to a problem you're facing or helps you to advance a goal.

Everything we do is relevant to our being who we came to the world to be. If it's not, it's time to stop doing that thing. I had a friend who used to shovel snow off the court so that he could play basketball.

He loved the game and how it made him feel so much that he would shovel snow in order to play. That's real love.

Loving what we do comes from a deep place within us. It's connected to our why, our values, our life purpose. Simon Sinek does a fabulous TED Talk on the power of why. He says customers are inspired to buy from people who connect their product to why. Your product is a mission for your purpose.

Sinek reminds us that Apple has astronomical sales because they believe in innovation and standing out from the crowd. He says people joined Martin Luther King in civil rights marches because of what they believed about America as land of the brave and free.

People buy a product or take a class or select a service because they're inspired by your beliefs, the good you seek to do. Sinek says, "People don't buy what you do, they buy why you do it." His book encourages us to *Start With Why*. In business relationships, when our beliefs match our clients' feeling for what's right or good or meaningful, they will very likely engage with us.

Every moment of our lives is relevant to being who we came to the world to be. Nothing is wasted. My Taoist teacher, Grand Master Nan Lu, says that every experience we have is moving us to a greater expression of our purpose.

Thinking about purpose as a driver, lens, or glue for our choices and experiences provides us with an infinite source of personal power. In fact, Hankel agrees with my Taoist teacher. He relates the power of our purpose to that of a black hole. He says physicists have discovered that nothing escapes black holes. They are massive forces that absorb whatever objects enter them and then they transform those objects.

Yeah. That's deep. Hankel encourages us to imagine that our purpose is drawing our thoughts, actions, our very identity into it. As such, our purpose is a source of transformation. It moves us to evolve who we are and how we live each day.

Purpose puts us on the beat. It's the heartbeat that came into the world with us. It's our natural rhythm. It's been marking time all of our lives, attracting us to those people, experiences, and choices that will lead to our greatest expression of self.

Your life is about honoring your greatness, doing good in the world, improving the human condition. Yes, you came to do great things in the world. Consider how your purpose creates rhythm for you. Here's an activity to help you stay in tune with your greatest expression of you.

Call to Action ~ Put Purpose In the Driver's Seat

1. Connect your work to your purpose
   a. In the previous section, you chose 1 – 2 words that describe your purpose.
   b. What are three missions you would undertake as a _______________ (Insert your 1 – 2 word description here)?
      i. Example: As a wellness educator, I would:
         1. design programs for business people who travel frequently so that they can maintain physical health, peace of mind, and bring their best to the world;
         2. create online courses that offer guidance on how to use everyday activities like walking and brushing your teeth to enhance health so that every person could access wellness;
         3. design programs that allow church groups members to pool their resources for a better quality program than each individual could get purchasing a single program.

2. About those things you don't really love doing:
   a. Pick 1 – 3 chores or activities that you don't really love but you get them done. Indicate how these activities help to support your why and help you to fulfill your purpose.
      i. I'm not in love with ____________ but it supports my purpose because ______________________________.
      ii. __________________ is not my favorite activity but I can see it helps me with my purpose by __________________.
      iii. Example: I'm not in love with cleaning my desk but it supports my purpose because when there is less clutter, I'm less distracted and I can be more creative. When there is order in my environment, my creative flow improves.

Spiritual Flexibility

An F-Word You'll Want to Keep Saying

I know you've heard people say that life is full of ups and downs. Better yet, the downs are as good for you as the ups. Yeah, I know. It's my Mama's blessings in disguise. I could not have predicted how important this idea would become to me as an entrepreneur.

But the practice of seeing everything as a blessing is also an example of something else that I learned from my Mama and elders. It's the F-Word--Faith. I watched a short video of Damon Brown, co-founder of a social networking site that brokers meetings between people who want to cuddle. No going all the way, just cuddling. Brown talked about one of his favorite books, *The Alchemist* by Paulo Coelho. I, too, love this book.

Brown likened the main character Santiago's journey to that of the entrepreneur. We're headed toward a goal, but we get lost, off track or sidetracked. Maybe we make a misstep, sometimes known as "the dreaded mistake." In other words, we go through changes.

Brown says, "Those moments when we seem the most lost," are actually the times when we discover our greatest treasures. We uncover our most useful insights. He points us to invisible power forces that sustain us along the way. Brown reminds us that being an entrepreneur is about having faith in our vision and trusting our journey.

Faith is a resource, hidden but very real. You may have your why, that is, your purpose. Moving from your why to your what, the product or service that you provide, requires faith. Failures become funnels that lead to actions that transform your work.

Faith reminds us to stay flexible. A zig can work as well as a zag. By focusing on the moment, we find ways to make our situation work for us. We use what we have to get where we want to go. Ride that zig all the way to our goal!

Faith is finding continuity between the invisible and the visible. The vision in our heart and mind is not visible. Yet, we trust in our purpose and our ability to bring it to life. Faith connects us to a deeper source of power. We can keep moving thoughtfully forward and feeling supported as we take each step.

I learned one of my most important lessons in self-trust from my Mama who taught me, "Follow your first mind." This was one of her reminders when I studied for exams. Parents have these mystical ways of leading us to our inner treasures. In addition to helping me access the knowledge for a test, this guidance took me deeper inside myself. It was a means for connecting with my own capacity to impact my path.

There are many things in life that can rock our faith, leave us questioning our life path. We wonder, "What was I thinking?" or "How did I get myself into this?" We may even say, "There's no way that I can get this done." Our work or efforts may not seem to be getting us anywhere. These are times when it seems that failure has stolen our faith.

In a *Vogue* interview, Jonathan Van Meter talked with Oprah about some of her ups and downs. One of the downs was the less than successful movie adaptation of Toni Morrison's *Beloved*. Winfrey talked about her "long plunge into food and depression and suppressing all my feelings." She was challenged again when she first launched Oprah Winfrey Network (OWN). She learned her audience wasn't interested in personal and spiritual development programming 24/7.

What did Oprah's take away from *Beloved* box office numbers? Detach. "Do the work as an offering, and then whatever happens, happens." What did she learn from launching OWN? Give people "snackables. You need snackable spirituality—snackable, digestible moments in an entertaining format, so people can receive it."

Two very important messages emerge from her experience. First, stay connected to why you do what you do, your purpose. Put your heart and soul into sharing your purpose through a particular mission. Do your best then let go. Trust that the outcome will only serve to help you and others to elevate.

Second, be flexible. There are an infinite number of ways that you can achieve your mission. Your project can work just as well through several small ventures, maybe better than it would as one big venture. Or as my elders often said, "There's more than one way to skin a cat." If there are obstacles on the road that you're on, you can go over or around them or you can take a different road.

In our careers or other areas of our lives, we sometimes make decisions that others do not understand. We take risks on ourselves. We believe in what we have to offer. We're driven by what we believe about our work. We're driven by our purpose.

We're not blind to the risks. We feel the fear and keep moving toward our goal. We're careful and we're daring, at the same time. It's that balance that keeps us alert, timely, and decisive.

Faith keeps our fire burning. So, here's what I've learned about having faith.

- Start before you're ready.
- Fail often and fail forward so that you can use the lessons you learn to build your dreams.
- Remember that you're capable. Be mindful of and grateful for all of those accomplishments, people and things that remind you of your abilities.
- Do the work, put energy into your work then, let go. Trust your vision. Trust your work. Trust yourself.

Take a leap of faith. Spread your wings. Fly.

"Faith is the substance of things hoped for,
the evidence of things not seen."
~ Hebrews 11:1

Call to Action ~ Full of Faith

1. Think of a time when your faith was challenged.
    a. Describe it. Remember what you felt went wrong and how you tried to fix it.
    b. What did you learn from this instance? What were the gifts that you took away?

2. Create a Full of Faith play list. These are the things that you have learned from those times that challenged your faith. These are the gifts of gratitude that will reignite your faith.
3. If you'd like them to be reminders, post them somewhere that you can see them.
4. Feel free to have fun with this.

Spiritual Connection

How Far Do You Want to Go?

If you want to go fast, go alone. If you want to go far, go together.
~ African Proverb

This proverb reminds me of the power of group energy. I used to work in pediatric HIV/AIDS as an educator for families and professionals. My organization was responsible for several programs each year. While there was a coordinator for every project, we worked as a team.

One of the best parts about the work was having the voices of people with different types of expertise (e.g. – nurses, psychologists, social workers, administrative assistants, physicians) add their knowledge to making a program happen. The other best part was that everyone felt responsible for every program, whether or not they were the coordinator.

I loved working with people who helped each other. Conversations in our office often sounded like this:

> "How's it going?"
>
> "Do you need any help?"
>
> "I came across this, I thought you could use it for the program on disclosure."
>
> "I met a family member on my trip to New Orleans. She might be great for our panel."

Yes, I know trying to reach consensus with a group can be challenging. But you can't even measure the power that comes from using each other's gifts and talents. You start to know that you can count on Sharon for creativity or Maggie for organization or Ama for packaging.

Many years ago, when studying John S. Mbiti's research on African spiritual traditions and philosophies, I learned the proverb, "I am because we are. Because we are therefore, I am." It resonated with me. I blended this idea into my life-beat bass. The bass keeps time, gives music its foundation yet creates a movement that makes things flow. Interdependence does the same for us. It strengthens our foundation and tunes us into the rhythm of purpose that keeps us moving, flowing and growing.

Working in groups shows us the power of multiple people shining in the brilliance of their purpose. In his description of "Ubuntu," Nobel Peace Prize winner Bishop Desmond Tutu offers one of the most compelling explanations of this concept. You may have seen Ubuntu in your neighborhood Whole Foods market. It was probably associated with current day sustainability, self-sufficiency, or collaboration projects aimed at sharing resources or improving health or creating the highest quality of life for all people. However, Ubuntu is an ancient concept that has so much to offer our modern world.

Bishop Tutu says, "There is no such thing as a solitary individual. A person is a person through other persons. We belong in the bundle of life. I want you to be all that you can be. I need you to be you so that I can be me." Interdependence is a catalyst for actualizing the greatest potential within each of us while simultaneously building a better world. The full realization of each individual purpose changes the whole, the whole world.

Simply put, I need you and you need me. Neither of us is deficient. Yet, each of us benefits when the other one does well. Like the Adinkra symbol Funtunfunefu-Denkyemfunfu represented by Siamese crocodiles who share one stomach, but they fight over food. The fight is useless because when one eats so does the other one. If we help each other, we help ourselves.

We can put the power of group energy to work for us every day in very simple ways. We can practice kindness. We all know how it feels when someone extends kindness to us. You know what it's like when your arms are full and someone holds a door for you. Or a friend meets you at your home with dinner after you've had a difficult day.

The power of these acts comes from how they make us feel. We feel good. And even better, we want to pass the good feeling on to another person. Kindness has a ripple effect. It just keeps on going. We want to share the positive energy that kindness brings.

Don't stop there. Build networks. When I was in elementary school, I learned a song with this verse, "No man is an island. No man stands alone." I'm reminded of the women of the Montgomery Bus Boycott. Many were domestic workers who used the buses daily to get to work. They were ordinary women who created extraordinary change. Their group commitment drew support from expected and unexpected sources.

Find like-minded people or people who have similar needs as you. Join groups or organizations where you feel nurtured and energized. Find groups that allow you to give and grow. Engage with those who invest in the power of community. Exchange your ideas and resources. Build partnerships.

Finally, we can ask for help. Yes. This one can be difficult for some of us. I know. Maybe we don't want to be burden or appear incompetent. But remember that there are so many people who would love to help us if we just give them a chance. Somebody will take your hand. You can help each other.

When we acknowledge each person's importance and capacity to provide support, we create community--an energy web that sustains and nurtures all of us. It works in the same way that earth and sunlight interact to grow a seed into a might oak.

What steps will you take to build community? How will you share the goodness of your heart with others? Here are a few ways you can put the power of spiritual connection to work for you:

Call to Action ~ Create Some Ripples

1. Commit intentional acts of kindness. You can be methodical or spontaneous about it.
    a. Make a list of kind things that you will do for people in your networks.

b. Set you mind on being kind as you move through you day. Before heading to bed, make a list of the kind things that you did for others.
c. These acts have to be something visible that the other person or persons will notice and thank you for doing.
d. When someone does something nice for you, pay it forward.

Call to Action ~ Power Circles

1. Identify your support networks. Think about who you can ask for help and who provides help even when you don't ask. You may have different networks for your various activities. Be intentional about noticing who's there for you. Here are some categories to consider:
   a. Sisterhood
   b. Childcare/Family support
   c. Self-care
   d. Career development
   e. Spiritual growth
   f. Emotional support
   g. Travel
   h. Entertainment

Let Your Life Outlive You

What will your legacy be?...
I am referring to what a person
has done with this life that God has given
to him or her....
Think now! Act now! To insure that your
legacy will be a positive contribution to
humanity and you will be remembered,
yes you will be remembered, on and on
and in eternity as God wills it.

~ Dr. Margaret Burroughs, Teacher, Artist,
Writer, Co-Founder DuSable Museum

Dr. Margaret Burroughs is the perfect role model for understanding the power of our connection to the world around us. She shines among those who use their craft, talent, and skill to build a better life and world. Teacher, writer, artist, museum co-founder, activist and more.

Her life is a prototype of spiritual energy that creates a win-win. She is a shining star for reciprocity, specifically, the notion that giving and receiving are one in the same.

Her work was personally rewarding. She used her work to enrich her community and address injustice. In turn, her contributions to her community and the world were personally rewarding. The circle is unbroken.

Dr. Burroughs' art, writings, and the museum she co-founded remain her living legacy. Her poem, "*What Will Your Legacy Be?*" affirms that each person is an important team member in this place that we call life.

Your business, your work, your actions with those you love will definitely change your life and your family for the better. You can change the world for the better, too.

Moving your work beyond the lines of your personal life opens you to a great source of fulfillment. Researchers say that sustained happiness does not come from the things that we accumulate. Lasting joy arises from fulfillment and meaning in our lives.

There are so many ways to make an impact. One of the ways that we can see this each day is among businesses that are finding ways to heal our world. One of my favorite publications/websites is *Conscious Company Media*. It focuses on sustainable business and using business as a force for good. And wouldn't you know, two women founded it. In addition to publishing uplifting stories about businesses that act as a force for good, they offer a range of educational events to support purpose-driven work and conscious leadership in business.

If Dr. Margaret Burroughs were here today, how would you respond to her question, "What Will Your Legacy Be?" Perhaps you're volunteering to teach entrepreneurship skills to girls. Maybe you donate a portion of your income or business proceeds to an organization that builds affordable housing. Maybe you're a yoga teacher who holds an annual yoga for peace event.

Take a moment. Think about the ways that you create a win-win in your community. Remember the rewarding feeling, the sense of fulfillment that you get when you give to others.

Win-wins tend to snowball. You continue to see ways to grow, share, and be nurtured in your exchange with others. You're creating a legacy. Your life will outlive you.

Spiritual Energy Chart

Spiritual Energy
Recharge, Renew, Replenish

Spiritual Wisdom	Identify your life purpose. Create meaning and fulfillment.
Spiritual Rhythm	Align your work and activities with your purpose.
Spiritual Flexibility	Have faith. Trust yourself through challenges and successes.
Spiritual Connection	Build strong networks. Create a legacy of good.

RECOVER YOUR

BODY
MIND
SPIRIT

Power Your Purpose

It takes energy to be who you came to the world to be. Your purpose requires power. In many cultures, this process begins during pregnancy. Sobonfu Somé describes a process where the elders and spiritual teachers gather and use their ancient wisdom to connect with the spirit before birth. It's called a hearing ritual where they learn the child's intention for coming into the world. Once the children are born, they are given names that reflect their purpose.

Imagine a world where every time you heard your name, you remembered all the good stuff that only you can bring can. You remembered that you came equipped to fulfill your purpose. That's some serious jet fuel for your life!

You are that significant. Your body, mind, and spirit are your team. Keep them ready and able to build your legacy. In this final section, we put it all together. Find some strategies for taking the opportunity to plug in to the power of you each day.

"Win at being you. It's the only job that only you can do."
~ Dr. Sandra Y. Lewis

Build to Win

We've all heard of a To-Do List. It's often all the stuff we have to make happen. Rarely do I see a list that includes self-care or energy management unless someone has been to a coach or training that emphasizes scheduling these activities.

I read a story in a newsletter about one very busy professor who diligently mapped out his day each morning. He scheduled in meetings, projects, and other work but also included naps, rest, and other self-care activities. Some might look at this and say it's good time management, but this is really good energy management. When our energy is good, we make the best use of our time. We take actions that are aligned with meaning and fulfillment.

So, let me introduce you to Daily Energy Wellness, or your DEW List. Think of your day as a combination of activity and recovery. During active periods, we're using energy. During recovery, we rest, restore, and replenish energy. Our ability to make the most of active periods hinges on our ability to rest and recover. The goal is to develop good habits and be flexible about the strategies that work across situations.

Treat these recommendations as guidelines to help you stay energized in your body, mind, and spirit. The aim is to help you tap your inner wisdom, create a life rhythm that works, maximize your resources, and connect with life in a way that renews your spirit and brings you fulfillment.

Get a Good Start to Your Day

Hal Elrod, author of *The Miracle Morning*, says how you start day is how you finish your day. You've been at rest, asleep; take time to reorient your body, mind, and spirit. Elrod says this can be accomplished in as little as six minutes. Feel free to start slowly. Once you feel the boost, you'll probably want more. Here's a combination of morning activities drawn from our Call to Action work.

- Take Two
    - The first 120 seconds of the day belong to you.
    - You're the first person to know that you're awake, so greet yourself and remind you of your purpose.

- Create a statement that acknowledges the super-person inside of you.
- Good morning, Abundance Educator. It's a great day to shine some light on how we can grow what we have into more of what we want.

- Digital Detox one hour
  - Skip the cellphone, computer, and other screens for the first hour of your day. Give your brain and body an opportunity to get into rhythm before you start responding.
- Do Your Body Good
  - Move in a way that brings your body joy
    - ★ This can be anything from light stretching to dancing to a full workout.
  - Eat well
    - ★ Some people prefer a light breakfast. Others like a big breakfast. Make choices that give your body what it needs to move through the next few hours with some ease.
- Light up your spirit
  - Read an inspirational quote or text.
  - Practice meditation.
  - Choose what works for you.

- Review your schedule
  - Look at the required activities and note the energy demands.
  - Make sure there are some recovery timeslots.
  - You will complete a thorough review each night so this should be quick each morning.
- Pick a feeling
  - You know the day's requirements. Decide how you want to feel throughout your day.

Mid-day Review

Most of us schedule lunch around the middle of the day. Our body is usually asking for more food. If we've been sedentary, it may be craving movement.

- Check in with yourself
  - Note your energy level
- Nurture your body
- Quiet your mind and get inspired
  - A deep easy breath can do the trick. Take a deep inhale and exhale.
  - Keep some positive quotes in easy access.
- Review your progress with your word for the day
  - Are you feeling the way you want to feel?

    - What shift can you make to get closer?
- Positive interactions
    - If possible, have lunch with someone who can bring some positive energy into your day. Remember to keep the cellphones invisible.

Pump Your Breaks™

Twice a day, take a moment to recharge and recover. I recommend a mid-morning and mid-afternoon break. Choose a replenishing activity or more than one that you can easily fit into your routine. You can take short breaks of 3 – 5 minutes or longer ones of 15 – 20 minutes. Below are a few ideas.

- Just breathe 3 – 5 minutes
- Breathe while listening to string music
- Meditation
- Meditate while listening to string music
- Meditate and repeat a simple mantra
- Walk
- Qigong
- Tai Chi
- Have a light snack or your favorite herbal tea. Breathe and really let yourself enjoy the flavor.

Get In The Bed Right™

This was my Mama's phrase for preparing for bed. If I was really tired, I might fall asleep in my clothes. My mother would stop by my room, wake me, and say, "Get in the bed right." This meant that I should undress, get into my pajamas, say my prayers, and get underneath the covers. Nowadays, this is called sleep hygiene. Our bodies need to know that we're retiring. While many of us do put on our pajamas and turn off the lights, we work until we simply pass out. Remember that passing out is not the same as going to sleep. We need a shut-down routine.

- Slow down
- Digital Detox 1 hour before bed
    - The bright lights from screens arouses our senses. Skip the cellphone, computer, and other screens for the last hour of your day. Allow your nervous system to slow down and get moving towards recovery and restoration.
    - If you use your computer or other device for reviewing your schedule for the next day, start your Digital Detox after completing your review.
- Review activities and prepare for the next day.
    - Take this slowly. Sit down and ease into it.

  - Some people like to let this wait until the morning. Others like to do it morning and evening. This double review is a good choice.
  - The evening review allows you to take your time, slowly begin disengaging from the days' activities, and start considering your energy needs. This means that you can have a quicker review the next morning. In this way, the morning review becomes somewhat of a treat. It's a way to connect with your plans and goals for the day.
  - As you review your schedule each evening, consider your energy needs and where you can fit in recovery time.
  - Get ready for the next day. Prepare clothes, food, organize paperwork, and do whatever you need to do to create a smooth rhythm the next morning.
- Optional: Brain Dump
  - If you have trouble getting your mind to slow down, you can write down all the ideas that are running through your head. It's best to use pen and paper. This way a device screen isn't overstimulating your brain activity.

- Practice gratitude
  - Think of 1 – 3 things you're grateful for that happened during the day.
  - You can write them down or include them in a short gratitude meditation. Simply take some deep breaths as you recall your experiences. Feel the gratitude spread all over you.
  - Be sure to reward yourself
    - ★ Think about what you did well today.
    - ★ Express gratitude and reward yourself for what you accomplished.
- Choose how you want to feel when you awaken
  - Refreshed
  - Ready
  - Fully charged
  - Rested
  - Energetic

This is a strategy for creating days where you flourish and find your flow. It's important to remember that we don't need to be busy all the time. Taking a break actually enhances creativity and productivity. We need space to think. Consider limiting your busy days to 4 – 5 per week. Create 2 – 3 days per week when you're doing less. Perhaps you take care of a small project, but you put more recovery time into your day. I call these low demand days. Below are some activities that may enhance recovery on these days.

1. Take a digital detox a few hours each day or for a whole day. Step away from email, phones, social media, etc. All the bells and whistles can be overstimulating. We get in the mode of responding to one thing after another or several things at once. We need some time to defragment, re-boot, and reorganize ourselves.
2. Take a walk outside. Get into nature. My god-sister calls these Wood Baths. They're like bubble baths except with trees and nature. They surround us with things that show us how much beauty and possibility exists in our world. We get to slow our pace, collect some oxygen from the trees, and breath in calmness. The stillness helps us find our own stillness. My goddaughter says nature walks and sitting with the trees help her put things into perspective. She feels like she's getting a big ol' hug from nature. You know the kind your grandma or some elder would give you. Time stood still when you got one of these loving hugs. Walking in nature reminds us that there's a rhythm

to everything. We will make the perfect move at the perfect time.

3. Meditate for longer periods. Take 15 – 20 minutes and get still in meditation. Meditation benefits every part of us. It changes your cells. Your cells start to show those qualities associated with longevity. Your body gets healthier and you get sharper. It's virtually brain food. Energize your brain with meditation. And here's one of the ways your smarty-pants phone can be an ally. Get a meditation app or play some soothing music or sounds on your phone. Breathe deeply and simply repeat I am peaceful and calm.
4. Dance. Often. Get into your groove. Nobody is watching. Let the music move you. Feel the freedom and joy of it. Release your tension with every beat. Feel good. Let joy and laughter be your super powers.

Be mindful as you greet and move through each day. There will be detours, obstacles, challenges. Or maybe you'll just discover a better way to get where you're going. Be flexible, ready to pivot.

Treat everything as information. Grand Master Lu says that our purpose seeks experiences that allow it to elevate. Stay connected to your reason for being. Everything is moving you to your greatness. Enjoy the ride.

Living in the Harmony Zone

One of the ways we mark time is in years. Each year there are a range of celebrations that invite us to begin anew. Many of us celebrate January 1 as the New Year and a few weeks later we may celebrate the Lunar New Year. We make resolutions, set intentions, and muster the energy to act on them. We ready our journals and rally our accountability partners. We meditate and map out our action plans.

At the Spring Equinox, astrologers celebrate their New Year. And on Easter, Christians around the world celebrate resurrection day, another opening to renewal, a fresh start. And we could probably add to this list of opportunities to "get new."

One of the most powerful benefits of renewal is momentum, increased motivation to go for a goal. Pursuing an opportunity can be like a car that gets a boost in speed when going downhill. With enough momentum, you don't need to accelerate. The car will simply coast without your effort. You can moderate the speed, but the car moves along pretty easily.

Feel that for a moment. Coasting. It's all downhill. No effort needed but there's a big gain. There's progress. Lots of progress.

Can you remember days or times when you felt like you were coasting through a project or realizing a goal? You had clarity. You were both peaceful and productive. The connections between the dots were clear. Your work was your reward. The more you created, the more productive you became.

Your brilliance was blazing. Old ideas morphed into new, better ideas and you knew exactly how to make them happen. Each step you took seemed to seamlessly connect to the next step. The right people seemed to call or show up at the right moment.

You found joy as things just seemed to "click." You were satisfied. Your life and interactions were a source of inspiration. Every day was a magical place full of possibility and action. Your morning run or meditation sent you to your journal with new ideas and strategies.

There were no wrong answers. Everything was information for the next level up or out. You were completely engrossed yet free to think, move, and act.

Athletes and many others call this "the zone." Well-known psychologist Mihaly Csikszentmihalyi calls it flow. He's written a great book about it. In one of his TED Talks, he shares seven different features of flow that very closely match my description.

Many people focus on how it shows up in our work or when we're pursuing our passion. But it's more than our ability to focus on our work or love what we do. It's also feeling the connection between what we do and the world around us. Csikzentmihalyi points out that thought leaders, engineers, and other innovators in flow focused on how their work could have a positive impact on other's lives. They were internally motivated by their love for the good in their work, their sense of social responsibility.

As Maat teaches us, harmony is the place where everything in your life works with everything else in your in your life. Your relationship with life and those in your life is clear and you're full of energy. I call it "The Harmony Zone." But sometimes, I don't have words for it. It's simply Mmmm. Or Hmmmm. I feel it. I hear it. I move with it.

In her TED Talk, Shonda Rhimes discusses her transformation during her *Year of Yes*. She talks about writing and the need to be in her creative space. She describes getting into her "hum." It's what makes the work good. It has a feel, a rhythm, sounds, light. The hum is "God's whisper right in my ear," she says.

Yes. Mmmm. Hmmmm.

Rhimes shares how she lost her hum. Overworking will silence your hum. When you burn out, there's no light or sound. "If the song of my heart ceases to play, can I survive in the silence?" Rhimes asks.

You may survive but you will not thrive. When we begin to think that the hum originates in the work or in the world or when external forces define it, we lose touch with its true source.

Rhimes acknowledges that the real hum is deeper than doing. It's being. It's love and joy. At its best, our work is really an expression of our deeper sense of meaning, our truth--that place inside where the hum and the Mmmm really live.

Work doesn't create the zone or the flow. The inner harmony, the sense of connection between who we are and what we're doing creates the flow, moves us into the zone. Then, we apply it in our work. Work that reflects our deepest joy feeds us and we feed it right back.

Think about how your work, family, and community responsibilities provide space for you to share your gifts, talents and passions. But don't stop there. Notice what you get back every time you share. Let yourself notice how your experiences stoke your inner fire. Feel it. This is your zone, your Harmony Zone.

Revive and recharge. Live in your Harmony Zone.

Connect to your truth and fulfill your purpose.
Order your steps to complete tasks and
accomplish your goals.
Focus and balance to maximize your resources.
Notice the gifts that you receive and be
grateful for your experience.
Recognize that you're building a legacy
Enjoy the harmony 'cause mmmm,
this feels right.

About the Author

Dr. Sandra Y. Lewis is on a mission to uplift women who elevate their purpose to transform their lives and the world. Maat, a feminine force of natural energy said to govern harmony in the universe, inspired her Life in 4-Part Harmony. Dr. Lewis says Maat shows us that it takes energy to get everything in our life to work with everything else in our life. Her love for wellness and spiritual healing arts, training as a clinical psychologist, and her own life stories blend into heart-felt strategies for personal energy management. Dr. Lewis's style encourages readers to feel that she's present as they work to improve vitality, productivity, and well-being. It's clear she believes the power of you is the force that makes your life the one you want to live.

Interior & Cover Design: Marty Marsh,
SupportedSelfPublishing.com

References

Amen, R. (2012). *A life centered life living Maat.* United States of America: Self-published digital version.

Bradberry, T, & Greaves. J. (2009). *Emotional intelligence 2.0.* San Diego, California: TalentSmart.

Clawson, J. G. S., & Newburg, D. (2009). *Powered by feel: How individuals, teams, and companies excel.* Singapore: World Scientific Publishing Company.

Elrod, H. (2012). *The miracle morning: The not-so-obvious secret guaranteed to transform your life before 8am.* United States of America: Hal Elrod.

Gawain, S. (1978). *Creative visualization.* Berkeley, California: Whatever Publishing.

Goleman, D. Emotional intelligence. http://www.danielgoleman.info/topics/emotional-intelligence/

Hankel, I. (2014). *Black hole focus.* United Kingdom: Capstone.

Huffington, A. (2016). *The sleep revolution.* New York: Harmony Books.

Huffington, A. (2014). *Thrive.* New York: Harmony Books.

Loeher, J., & Schwartz. (2005). *The power of full engagement.* New York: The Free Press.

Lu, N. with Schaplowsky, E. (2000). *Traditional Chinese medicine: A natural guide to weight loss that lasts.* New York: HarperCollins Publishers Inc.

Leitner, M., & Maslach, C. (2005). *Banishing burnout: Six strategies for improving your relationship with work.* San Francisco: Josey-Bass.

Meichenaum, D. (1985). *Stress inoculation training.* New York: Pergamon Press.

Misra, S., Cheng, L., Genevie, J., & Yuan, M. (2014) The iPhone Effect: The Quality of In-Person Social Interactions in the Presence of Mobile Devices. *Environment and Behavior, published online 1 July 2014.* doi: 10.1177/0013916514539755

Pert, C. B. with Marriott, N. (2006). *Everything you need to know to feel go(o)d.* Carlsbad, California: Hay House.

Rath, T. (2015). *Are you fully charged? -The three keys to energizing your work and life*. United States of America: Silicon Guild.

Rath, T. (2013). *Eat, move, sleep*. United States of America: Missionday Publishing.

Rhimes, S. TED Talk. *My Year of Yes*. https://www.youtube.com/watch?v=gmj-azFbpkA

Seligman, M. (2002). *Authentic happiness*. New York: Atria Paperback.

Sinek, S. (2009). *Start with why: How great leaders inspire everyone to take action*. New York: Penguin Group, Inc.

Yogi Ramacharaka. (2011). *Science of breath*. United States of America: Watchmaker Publishing.

www.ingramcontent.com/pod-product-compliance
Lightning Source LLC
Chambersburg PA
CBHW022110210326
41521CB00028B/184
* 9 7 8 1 9 3 7 3 9 2 0 1 7 *